Raising Resilient Kids Ages 3-7

Parenting Strategies for Big Feelings, Clear Boundaries, and Raising Kids Who Can Handle "No"

Samantha Macino, PMHNP

A Psychiatric Nurse Practitioner and Parent Advocate

Publisher: Macino Book Adventures, LLC

ISBN: 978-1-971759-19-7

Library of Congress Control Number: 2026910036

This book is intended for informational and educational purposes only. It is not intended to replace professional medical, psychological, or mental health advice, diagnosis, or treatment. Always seek the guidance of a qualified professional with any questions you may have regarding a child's development or behavior.

The author and publisher disclaim any liability arising directly or indirectly from the use or application of the information contained in this book.

Cover and interior design by Samantha Macino

Author: Samantha Macino, PMHNP

Table of Contents

How to Use This Book

Before you begin, here's how to get the most out of this book.
This book is designed to be both read and used. Some sections will give you understanding, while others will give you specific language, structure, and tools to use in real moments. You can move through it in order or return to specific chapters when certain challenges come up in your day-to-day life.

If you are feeling overwhelmed, start simple. Pick one area that feels hardest right now (mornings, bedtime, sibling conflict, or public meltdowns). Go to that chapter, choose one small strategy, and practice it consistently for a few days. You do not need to change everything at once. Small, steady changes create the most lasting results.
If mornings are hard → read Chapter 1
If behavior escalates → read Chapter 5
If emotions overwhelm → read Chapter 6
You will notice that some ideas repeat throughout the book. This is intentional. Parenting in real life is not about learning something at one time. It is about seeing it, practicing it, forgetting it, and returning to it again. Repetition helps these concepts become something you use, not just something you understand.

As you move through the chapters, you'll notice one framework woven throughout the book: HOLD.

- Hold Yourself
- Offer Accountability
- Lead with Clarity
- Develop Resilience

You do not need to memorize it. Over time, it will become more natural. If you ever need a quick reminder, you can refer to Appendix A for a simplified version.
Appendix B provides age-based scripts that can be especially helpful when you are in the moment and unsure what to say. Appendix C includes emotional regulation checklists and tools that can be used proactively, not

just during difficult moments. Appendix D includes the research that
supports the ideas in this book if you want to explore further.
Some days will feel easier than others, and that is part of the process.
There will be moments where you stay calm and steady, and moments
where you react more than you intended. That does not mean this
approach is not working. It means you are human.

If you lose patience, repair it. If a boundary slips, reset it. If a moment
escalates, return to steadiness as soon as you can. The goal is not
perfection. The goal is consistency over time.

As you move through this book, focus less on doing everything "right" and
more on becoming steadier in the moments that matter. That steadiness
is what your child learns from, and it is what builds resilience over time.

Introduction

The Parenting Shift We Cannot Ignore

It's 6:30 a.m. Socks are missing, the cereal spilled, and your child refuses to put on shoes as if footwear is a personal insult. You've repeated yourself three times, patience is thinning, and you wonder, "Will this ever get easier?" It will, but not magically, not overnight. Between ages 3-7, your child's emotions are big, logic is still developing, independence is emerging, and impulse control is inconsistent or absent. This stage is when patterns begin to form, for both of you. I've had mornings where I questioned every life choice that led me to arguing with a small human about socks.

If you're holding this book, you care about raising a child who feels loved, safe, and able to handle the word no. You also want to parent with warmth and structure, without yelling, over-negotiating, or burning out. You are someone seeking steadiness, and you understand resilience is built through calm, consistent parenting, not harsh control or passivity. The concepts we'll discuss will draw on developmental psychology, neuroscience, and behavioral science to offer effective, research-based parenting strategies and tools that actually work (Shonkoff, J. P., & Phillips, D. A., 2000). And along the way, you'll see that your child's brain is a bit like a construction zone: lots of scaffolding, lots of noise, and definitely not finished yet. We love our children deeply, and some days, liking them takes a little more work. I'm here to help you find your way back to that feeling.

How to Enjoy Your Child (Yes, Even at 6:30 a.m.)

In this book, you'll learn how to:
- Set clear boundaries without guilt.
- Establish connection and trust with your child.
- Stay regulated when your child is not.
- Use logical consequences effectively.

- Allow big feelings with validation and firm boundaries.
- Repair the relationship after losing your temper.
- Raise a child who can tolerate disappointment and hear "no" without falling apart.

Introducing HOLD

Throughout the book, you will use a simple framework called HOLD:
H — Hold Yourself: Regulate your own nervous system first.
O — Offer Accountability: Model repair and responsibility.
L — Lead with Clarity: Be brief, predictable, and firm.
D — Develop Resilience: Allow distress. Contain it. Stay steady.
HOLD is not a script to memorize. It's not something you recite like a parenting spell and hope for the best. We'll walk through HOLD several times so you can see how it works in real life; in the messy, unpredictable moments that happen between mornings, transitions, meltdowns, and bedtime. HOLD is something you embody, not something you perform. If you ever need a quick refresher, Appendix A includes a fridge-ready version you can glance at while someone is yelling about the wrong color cup.

Why This Book Is Different

Most parents are genuinely trying to do the right thing. You want your child to feel understood, supported, and emotionally safe. So, you validate feelings, stay patient, and you try to avoid power struggles. But the more you soften, the harder some moments seem to become. It's confusing, and it can make you question whether you're doing any of this "right."

Children need both structure and warmth to feel guided and secure. This book helps you hold that balance in the moments that matter most. Not perfectly, because no one is perfect, but consistently enough that your child learns what to expect from you.

As you read, you'll begin to understand why behavior often intensifies when you start holding limits, what's happening in the brain during those moments, and why your child's reaction does *not* mean something is wrong. You'll learn how to respond in a way that keeps your own emotions steady while keeping the boundary in place and the relationship intact.

The goal here isn't immediate compliance. The goal is long-term stability. Stability in your child's emotions, in their behavior, and in your relationship with them. You'll gain practical tools to move through hard moments with more clarity, less frustration, and a steadier sense of what to do when things get loud, messy, or overwhelming.

A Final Word Before We Begin

You will not implement HOLD perfectly, and there will be moments when you raise your voice, negotiate when you did not plan to, or feel stretched thin by the weight of everything you are carrying. None of that disqualifies you as a parent. Resilience is built through consistency and through repair after things don't go as planned. You are not becoming a different parent; you are becoming a steadier version of yourself.

This book is here to offer you clarity, practical tools, and reassurance that your steadiness truly matters, because that is what your child's developing brain needs most.

Let's begin.

Chapter 1

The Morning That Changed Everything

6:00 a.m.

It's dark outside. Snow has been falling, and the air looks sharp, cold enough that it stings when you breathe.

I'm already ten minutes behind, and I cannot be late again.

All we need to do is one simple thing: shoes on, out the door.

But my body feels heavy. My mind feels crowded. I'm running a mental checklist—lunches, backpack, keys, badge, gloves—while my hands move on autopilot. I'm grabbing lunches off the table, scanning the counter, thinking three steps ahead, because if I don't, everything feels like it might fall apart.

Carter is tired too. I can see it in the way he moves, slow and angry, almost glued to the floor. Every morning feels like walking uphill.

He protests everything: teeth brushing, clothing choices, socks. The same routine. The same resistance.

I've tried to make mornings easier. Clothes picked out the night before, simplified choices, predictable routines. Still, the protests arrive right on schedule. It's as if his body wakes up already braced for a fight.

I hate what this is doing to me. I feel drained before the day even starts.

I say it anyway, trying to stay calm, but we are out of time.

"Carter. Shoes on. It's time to go."

He sits on the floor like he's made of stone. Arms crossed. Then his feet start stomping.

"No. I'm not putting on my shoes!"

I feel my impatience climbing. My chest tightens. My jaw clenches. My shoulders rise.

In the past, I might have shoved the shoes into my bag and told myself we'd put them on later in the car. It worked, technically. We left the house. But today the snow, the freezing temperatures, and the physical strain of carrying him make that option harder. My exhaustion is loud in my body.

I drop to one knee to get on his level.

"It's time," I say. "To put on shoes."

He tries to kick me. My stomach drops. Now I'm not just late, I'm furious. I try to take a breath. I hear my own voice in my head: stay calm, regulate first.

Kick. Another kick.

Something snaps.

"Stop!" I yell. "Just put your shoes on! Why do you make every morning so hard?"

The words leave my mouth and I regret them immediately. Carter's eyes fill. His face crumples. He cries and kicks again.

I'm frozen in that awful space between anger and guilt, thinking what so many parents fear but rarely admit:

How did it get like this?

Understanding What Happened

This morning wasn't a moral failure. It was neurobiology in action. In this section, we'll briefly explain what is happening in the brain. If neurobiology isn't your cup of tea, that's okay. You can skip to the Crisis of Confidence.

When I lost my patience, it wasn't because I didn't care or didn't know better. It was because my nervous system was under stress (Shonkoff et al., 2009). The pressure I felt came from cognitive overload: time constraints, multitasking, anticipating work consequences, winter weather, and a child who was already resisting. All of it shifts how the brain functions.

When your brain is under stress, the prefrontal cortex, which is responsible for impulse control and rational thinking, becomes harder to access (Diamond, 2013). Meanwhile, the amygdala, the brain's alarm system, starts acting like someone leaned on the panic button (Diamond, 2013).

Here's what was happening beneath the surface. When you're running late, freezing, juggling tasks, and trying to guide a child who is pushing back, your brain reads those moments as threat signals. Your body shifts into a survival response. Your heart rate rises, your muscles tighten, and your focus narrows. Your tone may sharpen before your thinking brain has a chance to catch up. This isn't a character flaw. It's an automatic nervous system response, and unfortunately, your amygdala does not check your calendar before it reacts.

Carter's escalation made developmental sense too. Transitions from waking up to getting dressed and then rushing out the door are neurologically demanding for young children. His prefrontal cortex is still developing, and impulse control and cognitive flexibility are fragile under pressure. Resistance is often an attempt to feel some control. It's developmental self-assertion meeting limited regulation skills. In other words, his brain is still under construction, and the impulse-control department is definitely not the first section they finish.

Previous mornings also shaped this pattern. When the shoes were occasionally carried to the car instead of worn, it created intermittent reinforcement. From Carter's perspective, he learned that if he resisted long enough, the shoes might not need to go on his feet at all. This isn't defiance. It's learning. It's a predictable response to a pattern that was reinforced over time.

This morning, two dysregulated nervous systems collided under stress. Neither of us was being malicious. We were both overwhelmed.
Reinforcement: Why Inconsistency Backfires

Here we are going to explain intermittent reinforcement in further detail. As we have learned, behavior follows reinforcement. If crying sometimes changes your answer, crying becomes more likely. If arguing occasionally leads to negotiation, arguing becomes an effective strategy.

This pattern is called intermittent reinforcement. When a behavior is rewarded unpredictably, it becomes more persistent. This is much like a slot machine. The reward doesn't come every time, but it happens often enough to keep the behavior going. Unpredictable outcomes teach children to keep trying (Skinner, 1953).

When boundaries shift occasionally, children push harder because the pattern has worked before. This is not manipulation; it is learning. Consistency breaks that pattern. When the outcome becomes predictable, the need to escalate gradually decreases.

Quick example: if a child screams for candy and sometimes gets it, the screaming will continue. If the answer is consistently no, the screaming usually intensifies briefly (an extinction burst) and then fades. Practical takeaway: decide the boundary, state it clearly, and follow through. Expect a short period of increased protest; hold the line long enough for the pattern to change.

The Crisis of Confidence

If you're parenting a child ages 3-7, you know the pattern all too well. You start steady, your child resists, you escalate, and then you regret it. Underneath those moments are the quiet, nagging questions. Why is this so hard? Why won't my child just listen? Why do I feel out of control?

It helps to say this out loud. Love is not the problem, leadership is. When our priority becomes avoiding meltdowns at all costs, we unintentionally teach children to manage the environment instead of learning to manage their own emotions. Clear, steady leadership creates the space where real emotional regulation can begin.

This book is about a resilience shift. It's about moving from reacting to emotions to guiding your child through them with calm, clear authority. Ages 3-7 matter because this is when frustration tolerance, emotional regulation, and distress tolerance are forming. Comfort alone does not build these skills. Safe, steady limits do.

You will not be harsh, and you will not be cold. You will be consistent, predictable, and present. The combination of warmth plus structure is what helps a child learn that feelings can be big and still be manageable.

Parent Burnout Is Real

Parent burnout is real, and it affects how your nervous system responds in everyday moments. When you are exhausted, overstimulated, or carrying too much, your ability to stay calm and steady decreases, even when you know what to do. This is not a lack of love or effort. It is a reflection of capacity. Supporting yourself is not separate from supporting your child. It is part of what allows you to lead with steadiness.

Connection Builds the Brain

Resilience is what we see on the outside, but connection is what builds it underneath. Between ages 3-7, the brain is actively developing the systems responsible for emotional regulation, impulse control, and social understanding. These pathways are shaped by daily experience, and the brain is wired to expect consistent connection with caregivers.

When a child becomes distressed, a calm and present caregiver helps buffer that stress (Shonkoff et al., 2009). The child's body begins to settle, stress hormones decrease, and a sense of safety returns. Over time, these repeated moments of support and recovery form an internal blueprint for relationships (Bowlby, 1988). Children learn that big feelings can be handled, that discomfort does not break connection, and that repair is always possible.

Connection is not built only in difficult moments. It grows in ordinary interactions, especially through shared play and movement. When you laugh together, chase, build, or move side by side, you are strengthening the same relational pathways that support regulation and trust.

Perfection is not required. What matters most is repair (Sroufe et al., 2005). Each time you reconnect after a hard moment, you are building your child's resilience. Think of it as a slow, steady building process rather than a one-time fix. The small, consistent repairs are what create lasting stability.

Environmental Context Matters

Connection and movement are universal biological needs, but how they show up can look very different across cultures and families. Some communities emphasize shared caregiving, while others encourage early independence. Some families value close physical connection, while others support autonomy within a secure relationship. Secure attachment is not tied to one specific approach; it grows from predictability and responsiveness.

Movement also varies by environment. For some children it comes through outdoor work, dance, or sports; for others it shows up in imaginative play or household chores. The underlying principle stays the same. When children engage their bodies in meaningful ways, it supports regulation.

In more sedentary settings, movement often needs to be added on purpose. In highly stimulating environments, calm and steady connection becomes especially important. Understanding your context helps you apply these ideas in ways that actually fit your life, not someone else's parenting highlight reel.

Regardless of context, the core needs remain constant. Children do best with predictable relationships, consistent structure, and regular opportunities to move. Think of it as giving them the scaffolding their developing brains need: different styles, same foundation.

Calm Leadership Begins Here

Morning crises like Carter's are normal, predictable, and solvable. Your role is not to eliminate emotion. Your role is to hold yourself steady, offer accountability, lead with clarity, and help your child develop resilience. This is where HOLD begins in real life.

H — Hold Yourself. Regulate your nervous system first so you can respond rather than react.

O — Offer Accountability. Model repair and take responsibility when things go off course.

L — Lead with Clarity. Be brief, predictable, and firm so your child knows what to expect.

D — Develop Resilience. Allow distress, contain it, and stay steady so your child learns to tolerate discomfort.

Every moment is an opportunity to practice calm parenting. You do not need to change your personality; you need tools, clarity, and the reassurance that steadiness matters. Think of this as learning a new habit rather than performing a new identity. Small, consistent moves add up.

Parent Reflection

Think about a recent morning meltdown. Where did your regulation slip? Which step of HOLD would have helped most in that moment?

Write your answers down and revisit them as you practice calm parenting in real life.

Chapter 2

Regulate First: Why Your Nervous System Leads

The years between ages 3-7 are a neurodevelopmental crossroads. During this stage, the brain is rapidly organizing how it responds to stress, relationships, and emotional experience.

During this period, the brain is changing in ways that matter for everyday behavior:

- Executive function expands quickly.
- Impulse control is forming.
- Language capacity explodes.
- Emotional intensity stays high.
- Social awareness increases.
- The stress response system becomes more patterned.
- Synaptic density peaks and then begins pruning.

These shifts mean regulation pathways are either strengthened or left underdeveloped.

The prefrontal cortex, the part of the brain responsible for impulse control, flexible thinking, and decision-making, is still maturing while the emotional centers remain highly active. That imbalance means children feel big emotions long before they have the internal tools to manage them.

Children at this stage are deeply shaped by their environment. Repeated experiences wire the brain. When distress is met with calm, predictable support, the brain learns how to recover from stress. When distress is avoided, ignored, shamed, dismissed, or met with inconsistency, less helpful patterns form. Neither harsh control nor over-accommodation builds regulation. What supports development is calm, steady containment.

A quick reminder: your child's brain is doing the heavy lifting of growth, and your job is to be the steady scaffold. That does not mean you must be perfect. It means you get to practice showing up steady, more often than not. Think of it as coaching a very slow, very stubborn orchestra. Sometimes the instruments are out of tune, but the conductor's calm matters more than the perfect note.

What Containment Means in Practice

Containment is often misunderstood. It does not mean suppressing emotion or preventing a child from feeling upset. It means maintaining structure while allowing emotion to exist within it.

A contained moment includes three elements: the boundary remains in place, the adult remains regulated, and the adult remains close for support if needed.

The child may cry, protest, or resist, but the structure does not collapse. Over time, this repeated experience teaches the nervous system something essential, stressful moments can be handled without danger. That learning is what allows regulation in the child to develop.

Temperament and Differential Susceptibility

Not all children respond to their world in the same way. Research on temperament and differential susceptibility suggests that some children are biologically more sensitive to their environments (Belsky & Pluess, 2009). These children tend to react more strongly to stress, but they also benefit more from support. They may appear more intense, more reactive, or more emotionally expressive.

A highly sensitive child in a chaotic environment can struggle in ways that feel overwhelming. The same child in a predictable, supportive environment often shows remarkable growth. That makes parental steadiness even more important, not less. These children do especially well when caregivers provide:

- Predictable routines
- Reduced verbal overload
- Clear boundaries
- Sensory regulation through movement
- A calm parental tone

When those supports are consistent, many highly sensitive children grow into people with exceptional empathy, creativity, and insight. The sensitivity that can feel like a challenge in the moment often becomes a lifelong strength when it is met with steady care.

How Anxiety Develops

Anxiety rarely begins with panic. It usually begins with avoidance. Early behavioral inhibition combined with parental over-accommodation predicts higher anxiety later in childhood (Rubin et al., 2009; Lebowitz et al., 2014). When a child becomes distressed and a caregiver consistently removes the stressor, relief happens in the moment. The nervous system learns an unintended lesson, avoidance works.

Avoidance reduces discomfort right away, which is why it is so tempting. Over time, though, it teaches the brain that the feeling itself is dangerous. The nervous system begins to rely on avoidance as the primary strategy for relief, and that is how anxiety strengthens (Lebowitz et al., 2014).

Early Attachment and Structure

Early childhood does more than prepare a child for kindergarten. It shapes how their body and brain respond to stress. Long-term research shows that early attachment security is linked to lower rates of anxiety, depression, and relationship difficulties later in life. This is because early relationships help set the pattern for how the stress-response system works. When a child's distress is met with consistent, supportive care, their body learns how to recover (Shonkoff et al., 2009). Stress rises and settles in a healthy way, and emotional activation resolves. When distress is repeatedly ignored, met harshly, or handled unpredictably, the stress system can become dysregulated. Connection builds the ability to recover, and that ability is the foundation of resilience. Resilience is not the absence of stress. It is the ability to return to a steady state.

Structure strengthens a child's sense of safety. A common belief in modern parenting is that boundaries harm attachment, but research shows the opposite. Children do best when they experience both warmth and clear structure. Predictable boundaries reduce uncertainty, and uncertainty activates the brain's threat response. When children know that bedtime is consistent, hitting is not allowed, and screens have clear limits, their nervous systems can relax into that predictability, even if they protest in the moment. Protest does not mean a child feels unsafe. Inconsistency is what creates instability and chaos. Connection without structure creates uncertainty. Structure without connection creates distance. Children need both (Bowlby, 1988).

The Balance Between Attachment and Independence

Some parents worry that strong attachment will lead to dependency, but the research says the opposite. Securely attached children tend to explore more confidently because they carry an internal sense of safety with them. Connection supports independence. When a child trusts that the relationship remains steady, even during separation, they are better able to tolerate caregiver distance and try new things. This is why predictable separation helps reduce anxiety over time. Attachment does not limit independence. Attachment is what allows independence to grow. Think of attachment as the launchpad, not the leash. Attachment gives kids the confidence to take off.

Repair Protects Mental Health
No parent stays regulated all the time. Every family experiences moments of disconnection. What protects children is what happens after the disconnection. When a parent repairs by saying, "I raised my voice earlier. That wasn't okay," the child learns something deeply important: conflict can be handled, connection can be restored, and mistakes are manageable. Adults can become more regulated over time.
Research shows that relationships built on rupture and repair create stronger attachment security. A small, honest repair is more powerful than a perfect performance. You do not need to be a calm machine, you need to be a reliable human who comes back.

The Myth of Emotional Fragility

Many parents carry a quiet fear that if their child is upset, something must be wrong. This fear can lead to over-explaining, negotiating, or backing away from boundaries we know are needed.

Short periods of frustration within a steady, supportive relationship actually help strengthen the brain. This "positive stress" looks ordinary. It can look like a child crying because candy was denied, resisting bedtime, or arguing with a sibling. When a parent stays calm and holds the boundary, the child moves through stress and into recovery. That process of recovery is what builds resilience.

Protection of a child is not about removing all frustration. Bumps in the road are necessary for resilience building. Protection is about staying present and connected while your child learns to move through their frustrations.

The Beginning of the Resilience Shift

The real challenge in modern parenting is not a lack of love. It is a lack of steadiness. Many parents are deeply committed to supporting their children, yet still feel exhausted, uncertain, and worried about getting it wrong. The Resilience Shift is not about controlling children. It is about strengthening parental steadiness through calm leadership, predictable structure, and connection.

Now we begin to apply HOLD more intentionally. The HOLD framework brings together connection, structure, and movement in everyday moments, shaping how the child's brain grows and adapts.

Looking Ahead

Between ages 3-7, children are building the foundations of emotional regulation, resilience, and attachment. Their brains are learning what stress feels like, how recovery happens, and who stays present when emotions rise. In these moments, your steady presence matters far more than perfection. And yes, steadiness sometimes looks a lot like taking a deep breath while your child negotiates the exact shade of blue their socks must be.

Chapter 3
Why Boundaries Build Safety

Let me start with something practical.

It's 7:45 p.m. Bedtime is 8:00. Your child suddenly needs water. Then another hug. Then a different blanket. Then they remember something very important they must tell you right now. You feel the familiar pull—the one that whispers, *If I just give in one more time, this will end faster.*

Or you're in a grocery store. Your five-year-old wants candy. You say no. They drop to the floor. Everyone is watching. You feel heat rising in your face and the same tempting thought: *If I just buy it, we can leave.*

Or two siblings are fighting over a toy. You intervene. One screams, *"That's not fair!"* The other bursts into tears. You start explaining, and explaining, and explaining, because maybe if they understand enough, they'll calm down.

Boundaries aren't about being mean; they're about creating predictable limits that let a child's nervous system relax. Saying no with calm and follow-through teaches predictability.

So yes, the water request at 7:45 is inconvenient. So is the grocery-store meltdown. As well as the sibling fight. But each one is also a tiny training ground for safety. A chance to show that limits can coexist with warmth. The combination of steady boundaries plus steady connection, is what lets children feel safe enough to explore, fail, and try again.

The Moment Most Parents Miss

Most parents don't struggle with the rule itself. Bedtime is 8:00. No candy before dinner. We do not hit. The real challenge is holding the rule when the child reacts. The discomfort that follows: tears, anger, embarrassment, the fear of being judged. This is what pulls us toward negotiation, softening, or escalation. When that happens, children learn that boundaries shift when pushed.

For young children, testing limits is not an attempt to defeat you. It's a way to check safety. Their loud protest asks a simple question: Is this boundary consistent and reliable? If the answer is yes, their nervous system can relax. If the answer is no, uncertainty grows and escalation becomes the new habit.

Lead With Clarity

Lead with clarity is the L in HOLD. Clarity is not loud, harsh, or long. It is brief, predictable, and neutral. In practice it sounds like: *"It's bedtime."* *"The answer is no." "I will not let you hit."* One sentence, not five. Not a debate. Not a lecture.

Young children think concretely, and when emotions rise their ability to process language shrinks. The more words we use in those moments, the less they can take in. Long explanations often soothe our own discomfort more than they help the child learn. Clear parenting is simple because it works; simple does not mean easy.

What clear statements look like:

- State the limit once. Say the rule calmly: *"Coat on now."*
- Give one next step. *"Jacket on now. We leave in two minutes."*
- Keep your tone neutral. Even, steady voice; avoid sarcasm or moralizing.
- Offer choices inside the limit. *"Blue socks or green socks, then shoes."*
- Follow through. Clarity without follow-through teaches inconsistency.

Quick tips for staying clear

- Practice the script aloud when you're calm so it feels natural under stress.

- Save explanations for later. If a child needs more context, give it after they've settled.
- Be warm and brief. Fewer words, same care.

Practical moves to hold the line

- Name the moment. Use a short, calm script: *"It's bedtime. Water now, then lights out."*
- Offer a choice inside the limit. *"You can pick orange socks or yellow socks, then shoes."* Choices increase autonomy without collapsing the boundary.
- Be brief, then follow through. Say the limit, state the next step, and act. Long explanations fuel escalation.
- Plan for the extinction burst. Expect protests to intensify before they fade (this is normal, protests often get louder before they settle); decide how long you'll hold the line (e.g., 3-5 minutes) and stick to it.
- Repair quickly if you lose it. A short, honest repair resets trust. "I raised my voice. That wasn't okay. The rule is still the same."

Micro-scripts you can try

- Bedtime: *"Lights out at 8. Water now and one hug, then bed."*
- Leaving the house: *"Shoes on now. We will go in two minutes."*
- Public meltdown: *"No candy before dinner. We'll pick a fruit for later."*
- Sibling fight: *"Hands are for nice play. We'll take turns. Two minutes each."*

Why This Matters

These small moments are training grounds. Each time you hold a limit calmly, you teach predictability. Predictability lowers threat signaling in the brain and lets children move from activation to recovery. Over time, those tiny practices build steadiness, and steadiness is the foundation of resilience.

Parent Reflection

1. Think of the last time you explained too much and the moment escalated. Which micro-script above could you try instead? Write it down and say it once the next time.
2. Think of the last time you softened a limit. What pulled you? Which micro-script above could you try next? Write one sentence.

Guardrails: What HOLD Is Not

Before we move on, let's be clear about how to use HOLD. This framework is not a license for emotional distance, harshness, or shutting down a child's feelings. Calm, clear leadership only supports resilience when warmth remains present.

Key distinctions

- Clarity ≠ contempt. You can say no without eye-rolling, sarcasm, or dismissiveness.
- Firm ≠ loud. A raised voice usually signals your nervous system is stressed, not that the limit is stronger.
- Consistency ≠ rigidity. Predictable structure means boundaries don't collapse under pressure, not that you never adapt when it's genuinely needed.
- Boundary ≠ punishment. Boundaries protect predictability; punishment aims to create discomfort in response to behavior.
- Containment ≠ suppression. Children must be allowed to feel anger, sadness, and disappointment; we limit unsafe behavior, not emotion.

If you notice HOLD being used to silence, intimidate, or overpower, pause and return to Hold Yourself first. Leadership without regulation becomes control. Leadership with regulation creates safety. The goal is not compliance through fear but steadiness through predictability.

What Happens When You Hold the Line

Let's return to the grocery store. Your child begins to scream when you say no to candy, and you feel the pull to make the noise stop. Instead, you kneel down and respond calmly, *"I know you want candy. The answer is still no."* They cry harder, and this is often the moment parents begin to doubt themselves.

This is not a failure. It is a moment of nervous-system recalibration. When you remain steady, your child learns several things at once: the boundary stays consistent, their feelings are allowed, and the relationship remains secure. That combination of connection and firmness supports secure attachment.

Over time, repeated experiences like this build internal structure (Shonkoff, J. P., & Phillips, D. A., 2000). The limit is no longer something that has to be enforced from the outside. It becomes something the child begins to expect and eventually hold within themselves."

Put simply: holding the line teaches internal control. At first the limit is external and enforced by you; with repeated, calm containment it becomes an internal expectation for the child. That is how self-control develops.

What to expect in the moment

- Escalation is normal. Protests often intensify before they fade.
- Connection still matters. A brief, empathic phrase (*"I know you're upset"*) plus a calm limit communicates both safety and structure.
- Repair if needed. *"I raised my voice. That wasn't okay. The rule is still the same."*

A script to try

- Grocery store: *"I know you want a toy. The answer is no. When you're ready to walk, we'll go."*
- Why it works: The script names the feeling, states the limit once,

and gives the next step: no lecture, no bargaining.

The Long View

Each calm containment is a data point for your child's brain. Feelings can be big and still be manageable, limits are reliable, adults come back after upset. Over time, those data points form the internal scaffolding of self-regulation. Holding the line is not about winning a single moment; it's about teaching a child how to hold themselves and manage their emotions.

The Science Behind Boundaries

Decades of developmental research show that children do best in homes that combine warmth with structure. Psychologists call this pattern authoritative parenting.

Bridge to HOLD: This research underpins HOLD: warmth without collapse (Offer Accountability) plus predictable limits (Lead With Clarity) creates the conditions to develop resilience.

Parenting styles, compactly:

- **Authoritative:** Authoritative homes have warmth with consistent structure. This predicts stronger emotional regulation, better academics, lower anxiety, and higher social competence (Shonkoff & Phillips, 2000; Baumrind, 1967; Maccoby & Martin, 1983). Boundaries are not threats; they are stabilizers.
- **Permissive:** Permissive homes offer warmth but little consistent structure. Rules often shift under pressure. Children raised in these environments frequently struggle with lower frustration tolerance and lower impulse control. This is not because they are less loved, but because predictability is lower.
- **Authoritarian:** Authoritarian homes provide structure without warmth. Rules are rigid and often enforced through fear. Children may comply outwardly but experience higher anxiety and reduced emotional openness.

Why inconsistency backfires

- Intermittent reinforcement: When a child sometimes gets what they want after protesting, the behavior persists like a slot machine (Skinner, 1953).

What the science means for you

- Predictable limits and calm containment equals practice for the nervous system. Repeated, calm experiences of distress followed by recovery teach the brain that feelings are uncomfortable but not dangerous.
- Mechanism to outcomes: Those repeated recovery experiences are the pathway from early parenting to later emotional stability, academic success, and lower risk of anxiety (Shonkoff, J. P., & Phillips, D. A., 2000).

Parent Reflection

This week, pick one boundary to make predictable. Use one micro-script, expect an extinction burst, and note whether protests shorten after three tries. Small, consistent leadership builds the internal scaffolding children need to regulate themselves.

Boundaries and Anxiety

Boundaries shape how children learn to tolerate discomfort. When adults remove every frustration by smoothing every disappointment, avoiding meltdowns, or immediately accommodating distress, children lose chances to build tolerance. Anxiety grows through avoidance; resilience grows through supported containment.

When a child experiences disappointment and a calm adult stays present, the nervous system learns that it can handle big emotions. If a child learns that tears reliably remove limits, they may become more dependent on external soothing. If they learn that disappointment can be felt and supported without changing the boundary, their internal confidence grows.

Calm, consistent boundaries do not increase anxiety. Unpredictability does. Children may protest limits, but they rely on predictable boundaries for safety and stability.

Quick practice

- Name the feeling and restate the limit: *"I know you're upset. The answer is still no."*
- Stay present, then reconnect: Offer brief empathy during the moment and more connection once the child calms.
- Track progress: Notice whether protests shorten over repeated, consistent responses.

Parent Reflection

Think of one limit you tend to remove when your child gets upset. What would staying steady look like for one week? Write one sentence describing the micro-script you'll use.

The Emotional Work of Leadership

You're not failing, parenting is hard work. Feeling guilt, doubt, embarrassment, or anger when a child pushes back is normal. The emotional labor of leadership is learning to stay steady through those feelings so your child can practice tolerating theirs.

The hardest part of holding a boundary is not deciding the rule. It is staying steady through your child's reaction. Your child may cry, yell, or say they do not like you. You may feel guilt, doubt, embarrassment, or anger. None of this means the boundary was wrong. It means the boundary was felt.

Disappointment is not harmful. It is an opportunity to practice emotional tolerance. When you remain calm and consistent, that practice becomes a building block for resilience and emotional regulation. Over time, children learn something essential: their feelings can be big and the world around them remains steady.

How to stay steady

- Hold yourself first. Pause, take a breath, and notice your own reaction before responding.
- Name your feelings briefly. A short internal label like *"I'm frustrated"* reduces reactivity.
- Use a short, neutral script. State the limit once, then act: *"It's bedtime. Water now, then lights out."*
- Keep connection available. Offer a brief empathic phrase and return to connection once the child calms.
- Repair quickly if you lose it. A simple apology: *"I raised my voice. That wasn't okay. The rule is still the same."*

Parent Reflection

Think of the last time you softened a limit because you felt uncomfortable. What emotion pulled you? Write one sentence naming that feeling and one micro-script you will try next time.

Returning to the Bigger Picture

Internal steadiness must be matched by external steadiness. In short, keeping calm internal emotions while externally having clear limits, predictable follow-through, no negotiating during meltdowns, and not stepping back from boundaries under pressure. This is not rigid parenting; it is clear protective leadership.

This is what creates safety: having an adult in the room who is both kind and firm. Clarity sets the boundary. Consistency shows the boundary is reliable.

In the next chapter we'll go deeper into holding the line in real moments. We will cover practical language, natural consequences, and what to do when behavior escalates. Clarity is the foundation, consistency under pressure is where leadership is formed.

Parent Reflection

Take a moment to think about a boundary in your home that tends to fall apart: bedtime, screen time, leaving the park, or saying no to candy.

Ask yourself:

- Is the rule unclear, or is it hard for me to tolerate my child's reaction?
- What emotions come up when my child protests: guilt, embarrassment, frustration, doubt?
- When the boundary collapses, what usually happens right before it does?

Now imagine the moment again. Picture yourself stating the boundary calmly and briefly. Picture your child reacting. Picture yourself staying present, steady, and kind while the feeling passes. That steadiness is not harshness. Each time you hold a clear boundary while remaining emotionally available, your child learns: my feelings are allowed; the structure around me is reliable; reliability makes the world feel safe.

End-of-Chapter Parent Plan and Practice

1. Pick one boundary to practice this week (e.g., bedtime, leaving the park, no candy).
2. Write one micro-script you will use next time (exact words).
3. Set an extinction-burst window. Decide how long you will hold the line before checking in (e.g., 3-5 minutes).
4. Record one outcome after the first try: Did the protest shorten, stay the same, or lengthen? One sentence.
5. Prepare a repair phrase if you lose your cool: *"I raised my voice. That wasn't okay. The rule is still the same."*
6. Keep this plan visible (fridge, phone note). The goal is not to be unflappable; it's to be reliably human.

Chapter 4

Holding the Line When It's Hard

It's 8:02 p.m. Bedtime was 8:00. You've read two books, tucked your child in, said goodnight, and begun to leave.

"Wait. One more story."

"We already read two."

"I'm not tired."

"You need sleep."

"Just one more."

You pause. It's been a long day. He was cooperative earlier; **one more feels harmless.**

"Fine. One short one." You read it, say goodnight again, and stand up.

"I need water."

"You just had water."

"I'm still thirsty."

You sigh. **"Fine. One sip."** You return with water and sit back down.

"I forgot to tell you something."

"It can wait until morning."

"No, it can't." His voice rises. Your irritation builds.

"We are done. Go to sleep."

"I'm scared."

"You weren't scared five minutes ago." Tears follow. Frustration takes over. "If you don't go to sleep right now, you're not getting screen time tomorrow." Silence, then louder crying. You step into the hallway, heart pounding, wondering how bedtime has turned into a full negotiation you never agreed to join.

Where it shifted

The first change happened at **"Fine. One short one."** Not because an extra book is always a problem, but because the boundary moved in response to pressure. The next shift came with **"Fine. One sip."** Each small adjustment may seem insignificant, especially when you are just trying to get everyone to sleep. But together they teach a pattern: if I keep pushing, the boundary may move.

After that, irritation changed your tone. The final step was a delayed consequence that wasn't directly connected to the behavior and was unlikely to be followed through calmly.

This is how boundaries drift. It usually doesn't occur in one large moment, but through small, repeated inconsistencies.

Rebuilding the Scene with Clarity

Let's rewind the bedtime scene and show a clear, immediate approach.

Two books are finished. "Goodnight."
"One more story."

"We read two. It's bedtime."

The tone stays calm and neutral. No lecture, no long explanation. The goal is clarity and steadiness, not persuasion.

"I'm not tired."

"It's bedtime."

"I need water."

"You can have water in the morning. It's bedtime."

Crying begins. This is the moment of emotional endurance. The point where many boundaries give. Instead of changing course, you stay present.

"I know you want another book. It's bedtime."

If your child gets out of bed, move into calm follow-through: walk them back, restate the limit, and reduce interaction.

"It's bedtime."

No anger. No new explanation. Just consistent action. If leaving the bed continues, the response stays simple and directly connected: less attention in that moment, the door closed but not locked, engagement paused. The consequence is immediate and related, not a threat about tomorrow's screen time.

Result: The response is immediate, the message is clear, and the tone remains calm. Over time the pattern stabilizes because the structure is consistent.

Practical Steps to Use Tonight

- Decide the limit in advance. Know your micro-script before the moment.
- State the limit once, neutrally. *"It's bedtime."*
- Follow through immediately and calmly. Walk the child back, reduce attention, keep interaction brief.
- Avoid delayed threats. Don't promise tomorrow's punishment in the heat of the moment.
- Repair if you cave. *"I said yes when I meant no. I'm sorry. Tomorrow we'll try the bedtime plan again."*

Micro-scripts to try:

- *"We read two books. It's bedtime."*
- *"You can have water in the morning. It's bedtime."*
- *"I know you're upset. It's still bedtime."*
- *"It's bedtime. I'll sit with you for two minutes, then I'm out."*

Why Delayed Punishments Don't Work

Children ages 3 to 7 think concretely. Tomorrow feels like a completely different universe to a young child. Children link cause and effect in the moment. When a consequence is delayed until the next day, the connection between the behavior and the outcome weakens quickly.

By tomorrow:

- The emotional charge is gone.
- The original behavior feels distant.
- The lesson becomes unclear.

What remains is frustration, not learning. Delayed punishments also increase the chance consequences will be delivered in irritation rather than calm. When a consequence feels like retaliation, it builds resentment instead of regulation for the child.

Effective consequences for this age are:

- Immediate: Delivered close to the behavior.
- Predictable: Applied consistently.
- Proportionate: Matched to the misbehavior.
- Directly connected: Logically related to what happened.

This is why logical consequences that are short, immediate, and related are the primary discipline strategy for young children.

What Logical Consequences Actually Do

Logical consequences help children understand that their behavior produces predictable outcomes in a safe, structured way. When adults calmly follow through, children learn that caregivers mean what they say and that the structure around them remains the same.

The responses here are not punishments; they are boundary reinforcement.

- If a child throws a toy: the toy is put away.
- If a child hits: the play interaction pauses.
- If a child refuses to clean up: the activity ends.
- If screen time ends and the child refuses to turn it off: screen time is done for the day.

Each outcome is directly connected to the behavior, which helps children form internal rules: "If I do X, Y happens." That understanding is the foundation of self-regulation (Kazdin, 2008).

Emotional Endurance Is Still Required

Even when consequences are logical and immediate, children often escalate at first. This does not mean the consequence is wrong. It usually means their nervous system is adjusting to a new boundary. Your role is not to eliminate their reaction but to remain steady within it.

When you follow through calmly, without threats or shame, you communicate powerful messages: the structure is stable, big emotions are survivable, and the relationship remains secure. That consistent combination of clear limits and emotional safety builds resilience and emotional regulation over time.

You will not handle every moment perfectly, and some nights will feel like they lasted far longer than they should have. There will be times you threaten tomorrow's screen time, negotiate longer than intended, or escalate in frustration. That does not disqualify you as a strong parent. Repair matters. A short, accountable correction restores trust: *"I said no screen time tomorrow. I'm changing that. The rule is two books at bedtime, and we'll stick to that tonight."*

Logical Consequences vs. Punitive Consequences

Not all consequences are the same. A logical consequence is immediate, related to the behavior, proportionate, and calmly enforced. Its purpose is teaching: to show a clear link between action and outcome so a child can learn cause and effect.

- Immediate: Happens close to the behavior.
- Related: Directly connected to what the child did.
- Proportionate: Matches the scale of the behavior.
- Calmly enforced: Delivered without anger, humiliation, or threat.

A punitive consequence is typically delayed, unrelated, disproportionate, or delivered in anger. It's designed to cause discomfort rather than teach, and it often severs the link between behavior and outcome.

- Delayed and unrelated: "No birthday party this weekend" for not cleaning up.
- Disproportionate: Long, sweeping punishments for small missteps.
- Delivered in anger: Consequences that feel like retaliation.

Why the Distinction Matters

Logical consequences preserve predictability. Punitive consequences tend to create fear, resentment, and negotiation rather than genuine regulation (Kazdin, 2008). For ages 3-7, immediate, related consequences within a warm relationship are the most developmentally effective path to self-control.

The Litmus Test

Before enforcing a consequence, pause and run a quick internal check:

- Is this directly connected to the behavior?

- Is it happening now?
- Can I follow through calmly?
- Is this response teaching regulation, or simply releasing my frustration?

If you cannot enforce it with steadiness, regulate yourself first. Calm comes before clarity. When you respond from a grounded place, logical consequences help children build internal control. Punitive reactions driven by emotion tend to create external fear.

In the next chapter we will address moments when emotions rise even higher. We will cover public meltdowns, aggression, and words that feel personal. Holding the line in private is one challenge, holding it under pressure is another. The steadiness you are practicing now is what will make those moments under pressure feel more manageable.

Chapter 5

When Behavior Escalates

It's 7:55 p.m. Bedtime was 7:45. You've read two books, tucked in, kissed goodnight, and stood up. But your child calls, "Wait! One more story!" You pause. You've been firm all evening, but maybe one more won't matter. You read the story. You stand again. "Goodnight." Another request. A sip of water. Another delay. Frustration creeps in, your voice tightens, and irritation rises. By the time the tears turn into yelling, your heart pounds, and doubt floods in: *I've been consistent, why is this worse? Am I too strict? Am I harming the relationship?*

This chapter is about that exact moment: when the very changes you made to be clearer and calmer seem to make things worse. When boundaries shift, children test them to see if they're real. How you respond in that testing moment determines whether your leadership strengthens or wobbles.

The Extinction Burst

When a behavior that once worked suddenly stops producing the same result, it often intensifies before it decreases. This predictable pattern is called an extinction burst (Skinner, 1953; Kazdin, 2008). If crying used to earn one more book and now it does not, the nervous system tries harder. If arguing once led to negotiation and now it does not, the protest grows louder. This is not your child "getting worse." It's biology trying one last trick before the pattern fades, because the behavior worked in the past. Think of it as the child's final boss level: loud, dramatic, and short-lived if you don't hand over the extra life.

If you retreat during the burst, you teach the brain that pushing harder works. If you hold steady, the escalation usually peaks and then fades. The escalation itself is not the failure, stepping back from the boundary during escalation is.

When you begin holding boundaries more consistently, pushback is normal.

- How it looks: louder crying, bigger protests, more dramatic reactions, or repeated attempts to gain attention.
- Why it happens: the child is testing whether the previous pattern still applies; escalation is a short-term attempt to restore the old outcome.
- What to expect: a brief period of increased intensity followed by gradual decline if the boundary is held consistently. You may see new techniques and behaviors to get boundaries to shift. Hold steady and the negative behavior will lessen and stop.

How to respond in the moment

- Name the feeling, restate the limit: *"I know you're upset. The answer is still no."*
- Keep your window short and defined: decide how long you'll hold the line (e.g., 3-5 minutes) and stick to it.
- Offer connection after intensity: once the child begins to calm, briefly acknowledge the feeling and move on.

Quick script to try: *"I know you want candy. The answer is no. When you're ready to walk, we'll go."*

Public Meltdowns and the Pressure to Cave

Picture this: you say no to a toy in a store. Your child screams. People stare. Your face heats up. Everyone suddenly feels like they're watching, even if they're not. The easiest exit is to put the toy in the cart and sprint for the checkout. Relief is immediate. Lesson learned by the child: scream louder, get the toy. Not ideal.

Handled differently, the moment looks like this: you say no, the crying starts, you kneel, and calmly say, *"I know you're upset. The answer is still no."* You slow your breathing, keep your tone neutral, and if needed, carry your child out calmly. The storm feels huge in the moment, but the lesson is different: escalation does not move the boundary. Over time, meltdowns shorten, not because your child fears you, but because they trust the structure, and know the outcome.

Temperament Matters (and That's Okay)

Children vary. Some are easygoing; others are intense, persistent, or highly sensitive. Research shows that highly sensitive children react more to their environment, and they benefit more from calm, consistent parenting. In short, the kid who explodes the most often grows the most under steadiness. Temperament isn't a problem to fix; it's brain wiring to understand.

There will be moments when your child, in full fury, says, *"I hate you."* Ouch. That line hits parental fear of rejection like a rogue Lego. Remember, children reject limits long before they reject relationships. That phrase *"I hate you,"* is a feeling of overwhelm being expressed, not a verdict. Respond with warmth and clarity: *"I know you're mad, I love you, the answer is still no."* That combination: warmth without retreat, structure without hostility, is the heart of authoritative parenting.

Avoidance Worsens Anxiety

A different pattern emerges when a child experiences discomfort while a calm adult remains present and the expectation stays in place. The child feels the discomfort, moves through it, and eventually recovers. After this happens the brain encodes a new message: this feeling is uncomfortable, but it is not unsafe. When a child survives distress with relational support, the brain updates its expectations—this was uncomfortable, but it was not dangerous; I can do this again. This process, called inhibitory learning, helps reduce anxiety over time. Connection buffers stress, structure prevents avoidance, and movement regulates the body during exposure, and together these experiences reshape developmental pathways.

For example, a child who is nervous about preschool separation benefits more from, "I know you're nervous. I'll walk you in. I'll be back after lunch," than from, "Okay, we'll stay home today." The first response allows distress while providing support. The second response removes the challenge entirely.

How Regulation Becomes Internal

One of the most important psychological processes in early childhood is internalization. Internalization is how external guidance slowly becomes internal capacity (Vygotsky, 1978).

At first, regulation is entirely external. A caregiver says, *"It's okay. I'm here."* Over time, the child begins to whisper internally, *"It's okay."* This shift does not happen through lectures. If it did, parenting would feel much easier.

Each cycle of co-regulation strengthens communication between the emotional centers of the brain and regulatory networks in the prefrontal cortex. Gradually, the child needs less adult input to calm themselves. The child learns how to regulate on their own.

The same process applies to boundaries. What begins as, *"My parent won't let me hit,"* becomes, *"I don't hit."* External containment becomes internal restraint (Vygotsky, 1978).

Connection with a trusted adult accelerates this process because feeling safe lowers defensive oppositional behaviors and allows learning to occur. In short, steady presence plus consistent limits turns outside guidance into inside tools. And yes, it takes time. Think of it as slow, reliable training rather than a one-time lesson.

Child Physical Escalation

When escalation turns physical (hitting, throwing, or kicking), safety becomes the immediate priority. Calmly intervene with clear boundaries, such as, *"I won't let you hit,"* and, if necessary, use gentle physical blocking to prevent harm. Follow with an immediate, logical consequence:

remove the toy or pause the interaction. Avoid lectures, shame, or delayed punishments. The focus is on consistent structure, not drama. When aggression is met with steady, calm limits, children feel safer and learn that their actions do not control the environment, while the relationship remains secure.

When a child is very aggressive or displaying extreme outbursts, parents need strategies that prioritize safety, structure, and support, while also addressing the underlying causes of the behavior. Here's a structured approach:

1. Ensure Safety First

- Protect yourself, the child, and others without using harsh physical punishment.
- Use calm physical guidance if necessary (e.g., gently blocking a swing or redirecting hands) but avoid escalation or anger.
- Remove dangerous objects from the environment.

2. Implement Immediate, Logical Consequences

- Consequences should be directly connected to the behavior, immediate, and calm.
- Examples:
    - If the child is hitting or throwing toys/objects. The toy/object is removed or activity is paused.
    - If the child shows aggression toward siblings. Give the siblings separate spaces until calm.
- Avoid lecturing, shaming, or delayed punishments, which reinforce fear rather than regulation.

3. Stay Calm and Consistent

- Your emotional steadiness teaches the child that emotions are survivable and boundaries are predictable.
- Use simple, neutral language: *"I won't let you hit. The activity*

4. Identify Triggers

- Aggression often signals overwhelm, frustration, or difficulty expressing needs.
- Track patterns: time of day, activities, hunger, sleep, or transitions.
- Early intervention (offering choices, warnings, or calming tools) can prevent escalation.

5. Teach Regulation Skills

- Practice calming strategies when the child is calm: deep breathing, counting, or using a safe "calm corner." See Appendix C for calm corner ideas and emotional regulation tools.
- Model emotional regulation consistently.

6. Seek Professional Support

- If aggression is frequent, intense, or unsafe, consider:
  - Pediatrician or family doctor: rule out medical or developmental factors.
  - Child psychologist or licensed therapist: for behavioral strategies, anger management, or trauma-informed approaches.
  - Parenting support programs: programs like *Incredible Years* or *Triple P (Positive Parenting Program)* offer evidence-based guidance for managing challenging behaviors.
  - Parent coaching or behavioral consultation: individualized strategies for your child's temperament and needs.

7. Take Care of Yourself

- Managing aggression is stressful; consistent self-regulation helps your child feel safe.

- Seek support from trusted family, friends, or parent groups to prevent burnout.

With consistent, calm boundaries, logical consequences, and professional guidance when needed, even highly aggressive behaviors can be managed safely while teaching children self-control and resilience.

Lying: What It Means and How to Respond

As we talk about escalation and avoidance, it's important to understand one of the most common avoidance behaviors in early childhood: lying. When a child feels pressure, fears getting in trouble, or worries about disappointing you, their nervous system looks for the fastest way to reduce that discomfort. For many children, that strategy is lying.

Lying in early childhood is common, and it is not a character problem. It is part of development. Research shows that lying is connected to growing cognitive skills, including memory, impulse control, and the ability to understand another person's thoughts. As these skills develop, children begin to experiment with what is true, what is possible, and what might change the situation.

For many children, lying is not about deception. It is about avoidance. Children often lie to avoid getting in trouble, to avoid disappointment, or to protect their connection with you.

Why Lying Happens

In the moment, a child's brain is not thinking about honesty as a value. It is trying to solve a problem.

- "I don't want to get in trouble."
- "I don't want them to be upset with me."
- "I wish this didn't happen."

Lying is often the quickest way their developing brain can reduce pressure. It is important to understand that lying actually requires a higher level of thinking. Children who lie are using memory, imagination, and an emerging understanding of how other people think. In that way, lying can reflect developmental progress, not regression.

How Your Response Shapes Honesty

Your response to lying matters more than the lie itself. When children expect strong reactions, punishment, or shame, the brain learns that honesty is risky. When children experience calm, clear responses, honesty becomes safer over time (Rubin et al., 2009).

Research consistently shows that how adults respond to lying has a stronger impact on future honesty than punishment alone. Your steadiness, not the intensity of your reaction, is what teaches honesty over time (Rubin et al., 2009).

When a child is lying, stay calm and reduce pressure. Focus on understanding, not catching the lie.

You might say:

- "I'm not worried about getting you in trouble. I want to understand what happened."
- "Let's try that again honestly." "You're safe to tell me the truth."

Then hold the boundary if needed, separate from the lie. Instead of asking, 'Did you do this?' when you already know what happened, simply name what you saw. Questions like that create pressure and make lying more likely, while naming the behavior reduces pressure and helps honesty feel safer.

Honesty develops when children learn that:

- telling the truth does not damage connection
- mistakes can be handled
- adults stay steady, even when things go wrong

Over time, children begin to tolerate the discomfort of telling the truth instead of avoiding it.

Lying is not something you need to eliminate immediately. It is something you guide. As your child's brain develops, your calm, consistent responses help shift behavior from avoidance to honesty. This is not about forcing truth through pressure. It is about making truth safe enough to tell.

The Long View

Escalation can feel like regression, but it rarely is. When you shift your approach and hold boundaries consistently, the system often reacts strongly before it adapts. If you remain steady through extinction bursts, public meltdowns, or moments when your child says, *"I hate you,"* gradual changes begin to occur. Reliability grows, protests shorten, and intensity of negative behaviors decreases. These changes do not happen overnight, but they happen reliably. Children do not push boundaries to create chaos. They push to understand certainty. When consistency and calm structure hold firm, escalation naturally fades, and children learn that limits are safe, predictable, and trustworthy.

Returning to HOLD

When behavior escalates:

- H — Hold Yourself.
- O — Own Your Impact.
- L — Lead with Clarity.
- D — Develop Resilience.

Escalation itself is not the emergency, losing your steadiness is. Your calm presence during intense moments serves as the true intervention. Your clarity in the midst of chaos provides structure, and your consistency through extinction bursts teaches important lessons about regulation. In the next chapter, we will explore emotional containment more deeply. We will cover how to respond to big feelings without fixing, rescuing, or collapsing. Escalation is only one part of building resilience; developing emotional tolerance is the other. By holding both steady, you are helping your child learn to navigate emotions safely while strengthening self-regulation.

Parent Reflection

Take a moment to pause and reflect on the escalation patterns you've seen with your child. Think about a recent moment when you felt tested. When your child pushed, cried, or became defiant. What internal reactions occurred?

1. Notice Your Response: How did your body and mind react in the moment? Did you feel frustration, doubt, or fear of rejection? Recognizing your patterns is the first step in building steadiness.
2. Identify the Boundary: What limit were you holding? Was it clear, immediate, and directly connected to behavior? Reflecting on this helps you see where clarity may need reinforcement.
3. Consider the Outcome: Did your child escalate? How did the escalation resolve? Could the moment have been handled with calm, immediate follow-through instead of negotiation or delayed consequences?

4. Acknowledge Your Effort: Even when behavior intensifies, your steadiness matters. Recognize moments when you remained calm or returned to the boundary, even imperfectly. These are the moments where resilience is being built.

5. Plan for Next Time: Think about one situation where you can practice calm, consistent leadership this week. Visualize how you will respond, including the words, tone, and immediate logical consequences.

Chapter 6

Big Feelings Are Not Emergencies

There is a sound that can unsettle even the steadiest parent: the cry of a child in genuine distress. Not whining, not protesting, but deep sadness that makes your chest tighten and triggers the urge to fix it immediately. Your brain quickly moves into problem-solving mode, even when there isn't actually a problem to solve. Parents often unravel in these moments, not because of lack of discipline, but because of love. The key to calm, clear leadership is learning to distinguish between danger and discomfort. In this section, you will learn that big feelings are not emergencies.

When a child melts down, you are witnessing neurobiology in action. In early childhood, the amygdala, the brain's threat detector, is highly reactive to frustration, blocked goals, or perceived loss, while the prefrontal cortex, responsible for impulse control and emotional regulation, is still developing (Diamond, 2013). Logic rarely works during meltdowns; the emotional brain is active, and the reasoning brain is offline. Your calm, regulated presence provides crucial co-regulation, acting as an external regulator for their nervous system. Research shows that steady adult support reduces physiological arousal and accelerates recovery. This process is called relational buffering (Shonkoff et al., 2009). Calm containment does not eliminate emotion; it shortens its duration and strengthens the neural pathways between the amygdala and prefrontal cortex, helping children recover more efficiently over time. Resilience is not the absence of emotional activation. It is the ability to recover effectively. Resilience is built through repeated cycles of activation, containment, and return to emotional baseline. Big feelings are neural workouts, opportunities for children to learn regulation while feeling safe.

The Misinterpretation of Distress

When your child cries because you said no, it can feel alarming, and your nervous system may interpret it as a signal that something is wrong. In most everyday parenting moments, nothing is actually wrong. Children experience disappointment, frustration, anger, or overstimulation. These are normal emotions that are part of healthy development. Distress is not danger, and treating every surge of emotion as an emergency can unintentionally communicate that your child cannot handle their own feelings. Over time, this undermines resilience, and decreases the building of emotional regulation skills. Calm acknowledgment of struggles and containment support growth and emotional regulation.

What Is Distress Tolerance?

Distress tolerance is the ability to experience uncomfortable emotions without becoming overwhelmed or acting impulsively to eliminate them (Mischel et al., 1989). Think of distress tolerance as endurance, not suppression.

For adults, distress tolerance predicts:

- Emotional regulation
- Lower anxiety
- Lower depression
- Better relationship stability

For children, distress tolerance predicts:

- Frustration tolerance
- Reduced aggression
- Increased executive function
- Better long-term coping

Distress tolerance is built through lived experience.

How We Measure Frustration Tolerance in Young Children

Researchers use structured observation tasks to measure regulation. One well-known task is the "Snack Delay," where a child is given a preferred snack and instructed to wait until a bell rings before eating. Researchers observe:

- How long the child waits
- Whether they touch the snack
- How distressed they become
- Whether they distract themselves.
- Some children wait patiently. Others negotiate with the snack as if it might change its mind.

Another tool, the Multidimensional Assessment Profile of Disruptive Behavior (MAP-DB), measures irritability and emotional intensity across developmental ranges (Wakschlag et al., 2014). Both tools show children vary widely in frustration tolerance. Tolerance grows when adults provide consistent containment rather than immediate relief. Children develop the capacity to wait, endure, and regulate when they repeatedly experience structured waiting: not when waiting is removed.

The Internalization Process

Every time you hold a boundary and remain calm through your child's distress, subtle neurological changes occur. At first, regulation is external: you provide calm, structure, and a steady presence to stabilize their nervous system. Over repeated experiences, co-regulation strengthens neural pathways that support impulse control and emotional modulation, allowing external regulation to become internal regulation. The rule shifts from *"I behave because my parent is watching"* to *"I behave because I can manage myself."* This internalization only happens when discomfort is tolerated long enough for the brain to practice regulation. If every wave of frustration is removed immediately, the brain never develops this essential skill.

A Coaching Scenario: The Broken Crayon

Imagine a common scenario: your five-year-old is coloring when the crayon breaks, triggering immediate tears: *"It's ruined! I can't do it!"* Your instinct might be to fix it, replace it, or distract them. It's a very understandable instinct, especially when the situation feels bigger than the crayon itself. But a more effective approach follows three steps:

1. Hold Yourself: Pause and regulate your urge to rescue. Kneel, stay present, and calmly say, *"I see you're frustrated."*
2. Lead with Clarity: Acknowledge the situation without lecturing: *"The crayon broke. That's disappointing."*
3. Develop Resilience: Stay present, allowing the wave of emotion to pass without immediately fixing the problem. After the peak, guide problem-solving with gentle questions: *"What could we try?"*

This approach teaches your child to manage frustration, practice problem-solving under emotional pressure, and build tolerance over time.

Distinguishing Trauma from Normal Distress

Not all distress is trauma. Trauma involves overwhelming threat without support, while normal developmental distress involves frustration, disappointment, or emotional intensity within a safe, supportive relationship. A child crying because you said *"no"* to a toy is not experiencing trauma. Trauma occurs when:

- A child is repeatedly exposed to overwhelming fear
- A caregiver is consistently unavailable or frightening
- Emotional needs are chronically invalidated or ignored

Calm boundary enforcement does not meet this criteria. Consistent structure actually reduces anxiety because it increases predictability. Understanding this distinction helps parents remain confident rather than over-accommodating.

Anxiety Grows in Avoidance

Research shows that avoidance may reduce distress in the short term but strengthens anxiety long-term. When parents consistently remove triggers: skipping school, avoiding social situations, or eliminating frustration, the child's nervous system learns, *"I cannot handle this."* In contrast, steady support while allowing manageable discomfort teaches: *"I can survive this."* Accommodation is necessary at times, but over-reliance weakens resilience and limits self-regulation.

Big Feelings in Public

When your child cries loudly in a restaurant, it can feel intense, and the urge to quiet them immediately is strong. Instead, respond calmly: *"I see you're upset. We're staying seated."* The crying may continue briefly, and people may stare, which can spike your own nervous system. It can feel like the whole room just got quieter, even if it didn't. If you remain steady, your child's system recalibrates faster than if you respond with panic or shame. Big feelings are like waves: if contained consistently, they pass safely.

Emotional Containment

Emotional containment is not ignoring your child, minimizing feelings, or withholding comfort. True containment means remaining calm, allowing emotion to be expressed, and maintaining consistent structure. It looks like:

- *"I see you're upset."*
- *"The answer is still no."*
- *"I'm right here."*

Emotion is acknowledged, validated, boundaries remain intact, and the relationship stays secure. This combination of calm presence, clear limits, and connection builds resilience over time.

Why Parents Rush to Fix

Parents rush to fix situations because discomfort is uncomfortable, fear arises, or they want immediate peace. Resilience is not built in calm or avoidance. It is developed through supported discomfort. This is the essence of the **D** in HOLD: Develop Resilience. Resilience does not mean a child stops crying. It means they recover more quickly over time, frustration lasts minutes instead of hours, and expressions like *"I hate you"* shift more rapidly to connection. Children who practice distress tolerance early tend to show stronger executive function, lower anxiety, higher frustration tolerance, and healthier peer relationships. This is not because they were never upset, it's because they navigated distress safely with steady guidance and boundaries.

Returning to the Core Truth

Big feelings are not emergencies: they are opportunities to strengthen regulation, build internal structure, and increase resilience. Remaining calm while a child experiences distress is not ignoring them; it models survival and navigation of emotions. This ability to tolerate and recover from intense feelings forms the foundation of self-regulation.

Boundary Script Pattern for Parents

You can use this simple, repeatable script in any moment of big feelings:

1. **Hold Yourself**: Pause, regulate your nervous system, breathe.
2. **Acknowledge and Validate the Emotion**: *"I see you're upset/frustrated/angry/disapponted/sad."*
3. **State the Boundary Clearly**: *"The answer is still no,"* or *"We stay seated."*
4. **Provide Presence**: *"I'm right here with you."*
5. **Follow Through Calmly**: Enforce immediate, logical consequences if needed.

Example: A child screams in a store because they cannot have candy.

Parent: *"I see you're upset. The answer is still no. I'm right here with you."* (calm, neutral tone, steady body) Child continues: Parent maintains position, does not argue, repeat boundary once if needed.

Logical consequence: If a child attempts to grab candy, the parent removes access calmly.

This script keeps boundaries intact, models emotional regulation, and maintains connection.

Parent Reflection

- Think of a recent moment when your child had big feelings. How did you respond?
- Did you react with urgency, anger, or rescue, or did you stay calm and steady?
- How might you use the HOLD pattern next time to contain emotion while keeping boundaries?

Consider keeping a small journal of these moments. Over time, you will notice patterns, progress, and increased confidence in your ability to hold boundaries without escalating conflict.

Chapter 7

What Rupture Actually Is

You just raised your voice. Maybe it was sharper than intended, maybe faster than you would have preferred. Instantly, you feel it: the drop in your stomach, the surge of regret, the whisper of shame. In that moment, many parents make a second mistake: boundaries collapse. The first mistake is the initial escalation, the second is letting guilt or emotion dictate your response. True repair is not collapse. It is an act of leadership.

In every close relationship, ruptures happen. A rupture is a moment of disconnection, whether subtle like a harsh tone or dismissive comment, or more obvious, like yelling, overreacting, or withdrawing. These moments are inevitable and normal. Research on attachment shows that secure attachment is not built on perfect attunement, because perfect attunement does not exist. Attachment is built on cycles of rupture and repair. Children do not need flawless parents, they need responsive ones who can repair with calm, connection, and clear boundaries.

During moments of conflict, both parent and child experience nervous system activation. Stress hormones rise, heart rate increases, and the emotional atmosphere tightens. If no repair occurs, tension lingers and both remain unsettled. When repair happens through accountability, warmth, and reconnection, the nervous system begins to settle. Oxytocin, the hormone associated with connection, rises, while cortisol, the stress hormone, decreases. This process, known as stress recovery through relational repair, helps children internalize safety and strengthens trust over time. When ruptures occur without repair, relational insecurity and anxiety can grow.

The Difference Between Repair and Collapse

Repair is different from collapse, and the distinction matters. Collapse often sounds like:

- *"I'm the worst parent."*
- *"Please forgive me."*

These statements come from guilt but can unintentionally shift emotional responsibility onto the child, who may feel obligated to comfort the parent.

Repair, by contrast, models calm accountability while maintaining structure. It might sound like:

- *"I yelled. That wasn't okay."*
- *"I'm working on staying calm."*
  Followed by:
- *"The rule is still the same."*

This approach communicates warmth and honesty without retreating from leadership. It reconnects the relationship while preserving the stability children need.

A Post-Yell Protocol

If you lose your temper, follow these steps:

- Regulate yourself first. Do not attempt repair while still activated. Give yourself a moment to catch up to what just happened.
    - Pause.
    - Breathe.
    - Slow down.
- Name the behavior clearly.
    - *"I yelled."*
    - Short. Specific.
    - No justification.

- Take responsibility for your behavior and actions.
  - *"That wasn't the right way to handle it."*
  - No *"but."*
  - No blame-shifting.
  - Do not tell the child your behavior was their fault.
- Reaffirm the boundary.
  - *"It's still bedtime."*
  - Repair does not erase structure.
- Reconnect with your child.
  - *"I love you."*
  - Physical proximity if welcomed.
  - Repair does not require a long emotional conversation.
  - Repair requires clarity and steadiness.

This process can take under a minute. Repair requires clarity, steadiness, and accountability. Not a long conversation of explanation.

Accountability Models Self-Regulation

When parents model accountability, children learn:

- Mistakes are survivable.
- Emotions do not define identity.
- Repair is possible.

Children internalize what they observe. If they see defensiveness, they learn defensiveness. If they see accountability, they learn growth. Occasional moments of rupture do not undermine attachment. What undermines attachment is chronic unpredictability. Authority and attachment are not opposites. Clear parenting paired with thoughtful repair strengthens the relationship and teaches relational resilience (Tronick, 2007).

When Your Child Doesn't Want Repair

Sometimes, after a rupture, your child withdraws. They may turn away or refuse a hug. That can feel uncomfortable, especially when you are ready to reconnect. Do not force reconciliation. Instead, say: *"I'm here when you're ready."*

Repair is offered, not demanded. This models respect and autonomy. Over time, children will approach again, and your calm, regulated response reinforces safety.

Long-Term Trust Formation

Trust forms through repeated, predictable cycles:

1. Rupture: A moment of disconnection occurs.
2. Repair: Accountability and calm restoration happen.
3. Return: The relationship stabilizes and reliability grows.

When this cycle is reliable, children develop relational confidence. They learn:

- Conflict does not destroy connection.
- Emotions do not remove love.
- Authority is steady and predictable.

Over time, this long-term trust predicts lower anxiety, higher self-esteem, stronger peer relationships, and greater emotional openness. Repair strengthens resilience.

HOLD in Repair

H — Hold Yourself: Regulate before you respond.

O — Offer Accountability: Own your behavior.

L — Lead with Clarity: The boundary remains intact.

D — Develop Resilience: Show that relationships survive imperfection.

The Bigger Picture

You will lose control sometimes. What matters is what happens next. If you deny, blame, or collapse, instability grows. If you acknowledge, repair, and remain steady, trust grows. Resilient relationships are defined not by the absence of rupture, but by the reliability of repair.

Parent Reflection

Take a moment to reflect on your own experiences:

- Recall a recent moment when you lost steadiness. What did you do immediately afterward?
- How could you apply the Post-Yell Protocol next time?
- Are there patterns in your triggers that make ruptures more likely?
- How does your response model accountability and emotional regulation for your child?
- Consider a time your child withdrew after a conflict. How could you offer repair without forcing connection?

Write down your reflections. Awareness is the first step to turning challenging moments into opportunities for trust, resilience, and secure attachment.

Chapter 8

The Developing Brain

Children are not miniature adults. Their brains are still under construction, and many of the abilities we expect from them: self-control, patience, flexible thinking, and emotional regulation, are skills that develop slowly over time. When parents understand how the brain grows, children's behavior becomes easier to interpret. What may appear as defiance, stubbornness, or laziness is often a reflection of neurological immaturity. Children are not failing to behave well, they are still developing the brain structures that make consistent self-control possible (Shonkoff, J. P., & Phillips, D. A., 2000; Diamond, 2013).

As discussed in chapter 1, the part of the brain most responsible for judgment, planning, impulse control, and emotional regulation is the **prefrontal cortex**. This area develops gradually throughout childhood and continues maturing into early adulthood. Because of this, children rely heavily on the adults around them to provide the structure and stability their brains cannot yet generate on their own.

Parents often assume that if a child knows a rule, they should be able to follow it consistently. Brain development tells us something different. Knowing a rule and having the neurological capacity to follow it in the moment are not always the same thing. This is why a child can follow a rule perfectly in the morning and seem to forget it entirely by the afternoon.

When adults remain steady, they act as an external regulator for the child's developing nervous system. Over time, the structure parents provide is gradually internalized by the child's brain.

Executive Function Skills

Many of the daily struggles parents encounter are related to executive function, a group of brain-based skills that allow children to manage behavior and emotions effectively.

Executive function includes:

- Working memory: the ability to hold information in mind while completing a task.
- Inhibitory control: the ability to pause before acting on an impulse.
- Cognitive flexibility: the ability to shift thinking, adjust to change, and recover from disappointment.

These skills do not appear overnight. They develop slowly, and often unevenly. Children rely on adults to help bridge the gap between what they know and what they can consistently do.

Why Structure Supports the Brain

Structure is not about control; it is about support. Clear routines and predictable expectations reduce the number of decisions a child's brain must make throughout the day. When the environment provides stability, the developing brain can focus more energy on learning and growth rather than constant problem-solving.

Helpful forms of structure include:

- consistent daily routines
- clear expectations that are stated simply
- predictable consequences
- advance warnings before transitions
- calm reminders instead of repeated lectures

Structure acts as a scaffold for the developing brain. As children grow and their executive function strengthens, they gradually need less external support.

The Parent as the External Prefrontal Cortex

In the early years, parents function as the child's external prefrontal cortex. When a child becomes overwhelmed, the adult's calm presence helps the nervous system settle. When a child struggles to make a wise decision, the adult provides guidance. When emotions run high, the adult helps organize the moment.

This does not mean solving every problem for the child. Instead, it means providing enough stability that the child's brain can slowly learn how to manage these tasks independently. Children borrow regulation from adults long before they can generate it themselves.

Common Developmental Struggles

Many behaviors that concern parents are actually normal expressions of a developing brain.

Children may struggle with:

- stopping an activity they enjoy
- tolerating frustration
- transitioning between tasks, especially when the transition involves stopping something they enjoy
- remembering multi-step instructions
- managing strong emotions
- accepting limits

These challenges are not signs that a child is failing. They are signs that the brain is still practicing. When parents respond with calm structure instead of anger or shame, children are given the opportunity to strengthen the skills they are still learning.

Recovery Matters More Than Perfection

No parent responds perfectly every time. There will be moments when frustration rises, voices get louder than intended, or patience runs thin. Children benefit most from an environment where boundaries are clear, emotions are acknowledged, and adults remain committed to guiding them through difficult moments.

The developing brain requires consistent safety, structure, and connection.

Play Is Emotional Practice

Play is often mistaken for optional downtime, but from a neuroscience perspective it is how children practice regulation. Research in affective neuroscience identifies play as a core emotional system that supports social brain development (Panksepp, 2007). Rough and tumble play, in particular, teaches a crucial skill: how to feel excitement and intensity without becoming aggressive.

Play naturally includes excitement, social feedback, boundary testing, and emotional shifts. In those moments children move in and out of activation and regulation. They run, pause, laugh, and reset. That back and forth is how the brain learns flexibility.

When caregivers join in, especially during physical play, they provide real-time guidance. Simple cues like "too hard," "pause," or "my turn" help children understand limits while staying engaged. Those repeated interactions strengthen the brain's ability to regulate within relationships. Play is not separate from connection. Play is connection in motion. Yes, sometimes play looks like chaos; sometimes it looks like a wrestling match in the living room. Either way, it is doing the hard work of building a child's emotional toolbox.

Movement Organizes the Nervous System

Connection helps organize the relational brain, and movement organizes the body's regulation systems. Early skills like balance, body awareness, and touch directly support attention, coordination, and emotional steadiness. When those systems are practiced, a child's ability to stay calm and focused improves.

Activities such as jumping, climbing, rough-and-tumble play, and interactive storytelling activate the pathways that support regulation. Even short bursts of movement after screen time or during transitions can reset a child's emotional state and support more flexible, regulated behavior. Movement does not have to be elaborate; a quick dance in the kitchen or a five-minute animal walk across the living room can make a real difference.

Parent tip: pair movement with connection. Chase, dance, wrestle, or tell stories together. When children experience energy and excitement within a safe, connected relationship, it strengthens both neural flexibility and emotional resilience.

Movement as Emotional Medicine

Movement supports the brain just as much as it supports the body. Physical activity plays a significant role in emotional and cognitive development. It supports attention, impulse control, working memory, and emotional stability. Movement increases brain-derived neurotrophic factor, a protein that helps the brain grow and adapt. It also strengthens dopamine systems related to motivation and reward and increases serotonin, which supports a more stable mood (Ratey, 2008; Best, 2010).

Some types of movement are especially calming. Activities that involve pushing, pulling, or carrying weight activate deep pressure receptors in the body and help settle the nervous system. This can look like climbing, jumping, animal walks, carrying groceries, helping with laundry, or even pushing against a wall. Yes, helping with the laundry counts as therapy.

These are not just ways to burn energy. They are powerful tools for regulation. When movement is combined with connection, its impact deepens. A child who is moving while engaged with a caregiver experiences both physical regulation and emotional safety. Shared eye contact, laughter, or playful cues make the emotional benefit even stronger. Movement helps organize the body, connection helps organize emotion, and together they support a steadier, more regulated nervous system.

When Children Need More Support

While all children develop along the same general neurological pathway, some children require additional support as their brains grow. Differences in attention, sensory processing, learning style, or early life stress can influence how a child experiences the world and responds to guidance.

In these situations, the principles of calm parenting remain the same. What changes is how that leadership is delivered.

In the next chapter, we will explore how parents can apply these same foundational principles when children are navigating neurodiversity, heightened stress responses, or trauma-related challenges. Understanding these differences allows parents to respond with greater clarity, compassion, and effectiveness.

Parent Reflection

Take a moment to consider your child's development through the lens of the growing brain.

Reflect on the following questions:

- Which executive function skill seems hardest for your child right now?
    - remembering instructions
    - controlling impulses
    - adjusting when plans change
- During what parts of the day does your child struggle the most?
    - mornings

  - transitions
  - evenings
  - busy environments
- What kind of support might your child's developing brain need more of right now?

Possible adjustments might include:

- simplifying instructions
- offering clearer routines
- giving transition warnings
- providing calm reminders instead of repeated corrections

Choose **one small adjustment** you will try this week.

Children benefit most from adults who remain curious about development and willing to adjust their leadership as the brain grows.

Chapter 9

Trauma Informed Care and Understanding Neurodiversity

Some parenting moments feel confusing in a different way. You set a clear boundary, stay calm, and follow through, yet your child's reaction feels much bigger than the situation itself. This chapter helps you read the signal beneath the noise:

- When a child's reaction is louder, longer, or stranger than expected.
- What the nervous system is doing
- How trauma or neurodiversity can change the rules of the game
- How to hold the line with both authority and compassion.

This chapter will teach you how to do all this while you're still wearing yesterday's coffee stain like a badge of honor.

The Nervous System Is Not Trying to Be Difficult

When a child's alarm system fires, thinking goes offline and survival responses take over. That looks like yelling, bolting, shutting down, or hyperactivity, not deliberate misbehavior. The practical implication is simple: behavior is communication. The louder the behavior, the louder the message (Shonkoff et al., 2009).

What's happening biologically

- The prefrontal cortex (thinking brain) is still developing in ages 3-7.
- The amygdala and brainstem (alarm systems) are fast and reflexive.
- Under stress, the body prioritizes immediate safety over reasoning.

Parent move

- Regulate first. Slow your breath, lower your voice, and reduce motion. Your calm is the single most effective tool you have in that moment.

Micro-script

- *"I see you're really sad/angry/frustrated/disappointed. I'm right here. The rule is still the same."*

Short vignette: You tell your child no to a second cookie. They scream like you've announced the end of the world. Your instinct is to explain. Instead: breathe, kneel, one sentence, and a small regulation offer: a five-minute stomp session or a hug if they want it. The boundary stands; the body gets help.

Parent exercise

- Practice the pause: Next time you feel your chest tighten, count silently to four, exhale for four, and say one sentence. Write down the sentence you'll use in a meltdown and practice it aloud three times this week.

Trauma Informed Parenting Safety and Structure

Trauma changes how a child's nervous system expects the world. Predictability and emotional safety are the antidote, not removing limits. Trauma-informed parenting asks a single question: Does this child feel safe? If the answer is no, behavior will keep asking that question until safety is clear.

Core principles

- Predictability matters. Routines reduce threat signals.

- Connection comes before correction. When a child is dysregulated, repair the relationship first.
- Boundaries are safety. Limits tell the nervous system what to expect.

Practical moves

- Give advance warnings for transitions.
- Use short, calm language.
- Offer a safe place or a predictable ritual to return to after getting upset.

Micro-script

- *"That felt scary. We'll stay here until you feel safe."*

Humor break: If your child treats your calm voice like a rare podcast episode, consider yourself lucky, you've become premium content.

Parent exercise

- Create a safety script: Write a 10-word script you will use when your child is emotionally struggling (e.g., *"You're safe. I'm here. We'll wait until you're ready."*). Tape it to the fridge and read it aloud once a day until it feels natural.

Neurodiversity: Different Wiring, Different Supports

Neurodiversity means different wiring, not bad parenting. ADHD, autism, sensory processing differences, and high sensitivity change how children experience transitions, noise, touch, and surprise. The goal is not to "fix" the child but to adapt the environment to the wiring.

Key scaffolds

- Movement breaks (heavy work like carrying laundry) are regulation, not bribery.

- Visual schedules reduce cognitive load.
- One-step instructions and timers help working memory and impulse control.
- Sensory tools (fidgets, weighted blankets, noise-reducing headphones) are legitimate regulation tools.

Micro-script for transitions

- *"Five more minutes. Timer on. When it rings, we go."*

Practical example: If a child with sensory sensitivity refuses shoes, try a short sensory warm-up (jumping jacks or a sock-scrunch game) before the shoe step. The body gets primed and the brain can cooperate.

Parent exercise

- Sensory audit: For one week, note three times your child seems dysregulated and what sensory input was present (noise, texture, light). Identify one small environmental change to try the next day.

When Intensity Is High

High intensity responses require a clear hierarchy: safety, containment, connection, then teaching. The immediate goal is to keep everyone safe and reduce escalation; the later goal is learning.

Immediate priorities

1. Safety: protect everyone without shaming.
2. Containment: neutral language, minimal words.
3. Connection: proximity or calm presence, not a lecture.
4. Teaching: brief, concrete learning after the child is calm.

If aggression occurs

- Calmly block or remove the child from the situation.

- State the boundary once.
- Apply an immediate, logical consequence (pause the activity).
- Repair quickly when calm.

Micro-script for aggression

- *"I won't let you hit. We stop playing until our hands are gentle."*

As discussed earlier, delayed punishments don't work. Long, delayed punishments (e.g., "no TV next week") disconnect the consequence from the behavior and teach nothing. Immediate, related consequences teach cause and effect.

Parent exercise

- Calm-down plan: Create a one-page plan with three safe places in your home, two calming activities, and one immediate consequence you will use for hitting or biting. Practice the plan with a role play.

Adapting HOLD for Trauma and Neurodiversity

HOLD is flexible. When a child has trauma or neurodivergence, each step needs small adaptations.

H — Hold Yourself: Your regulation is the external prefrontal cortex. Use breath, posture, and a one-sentence anchor. If you need to step away for 30 seconds to breathe, do it and come back.

O — Offer Accountability: Model repair quickly and briefly. *"I raised my voice. That wasn't okay. The rule is still the same."* Keep the apology short and the boundary intact.

L — Lead with Clarity: Use fewer words, more predictability. Visuals, timers, and consistent phrasing reduce cognitive load.

D — Develop Resilience: Scaffold distress tolerance with supports (movement, sensory tools, stepwise exposure) rather than removing every challenge. Small, repeated exposures with support teach the nervous system that discomfort is survivable.

Example adaptation For a child who shuts down when overwhelmed, replace long verbal repairs with a calm touch, a visual card that says "I'm sorry," and a short, predictable reconnection ritual like two deep breaths together.

Parent exercise

- HOLD rehearsal: Pick one common trigger (bedtime, leaving the park). Write a 3-line script for each HOLD step. Practice it aloud twice this week until it feels like a reflex.

When to Seek Extra Help and What That Looks Like

Asking for help is leadership, not failure. Consider professional input if you see persistent, impairing, or unsafe behavior; regression; self-injury; or anxiety that prevents daily functioning.

Who can help

- Occupational therapists for sensory needs.
- Behavioral consultants for consistent strategies.
- Trauma-informed therapists for attachment and regulation work.
- Developmental pediatricians for diagnostic clarity.

How to talk about help with your child

- Micro-script: *"This is bigger than I can handle alone right now. I'm going to get help so we can do better for you."* (Use age-appropriate language.)

Parent exercise

- Help checklist: If one or more of these are true, consider a consult: behavior is getting worse over months; school reports consistent difficulty; safety is a concern; daily routines are impossible. Make the call this month, you'll feel better after the first conversation.

Practical Toolbox Ready to Use

- Two-sentence meltdown script: *"I see you're upset. The answer is still no. I'm right here."*
- Transition aid: Visual timer + one choice + immediate follow-through.
- Movement prescription: 3-5 minutes of heavy work before a demanding task.
- Low-capacity version: One breath, one sentence, one steady action. That's enough.
- Repair script: *"I raised my voice. That wasn't okay. I'm sorry. The rule is still the same."*

Quick humor: If your child's nervous system were a TV show, some days it would feel dramatic and unpredictable. Your role is to keep the set safe, the script short, and the commercial breaks predictable.

Parent exercise

1. One-line scripts: Write five one-line scripts for common moments (no to candy, bedtime, leaving the playground, sibling fight, refusal to wear coat). Practice them.
2. Sensory kit: Put together a small bag with a chewy, a fidget, a small weighted item, and a visual timer. Keep it by the door.
3. Repair log: For one week, note each time you repair after a rupture. What did you say? How did your child respond? Celebrate the small wins.

Final Note

You will not always get this right. Some days you'll be the calm lighthouse and other days you'll be a flickering candle. Both are human. The difference is repair and repetition. Keep the routines, keep the boundaries, and keep showing up — even when the show is messy. Over time, the drama gets shorter, the script gets simpler, and the applause (quietly) grows.

Two lines to carry with you:

- *"Some parenting moments feel confusing in a different way. You set a clear boundary, stay calm, and follow through, yet your child's reaction feels much bigger than the situation itself."*
- *"Resilience is built in the small, repeated repairs, not in perfection."*

Chapter 10
Raising a Child Who Can Handle *"No"*

At some point every parent asks a quiet question: *is this working?* Not in the middle of a grocery-store meltdown or a bedtime standoff, but later, when the house is quiet and doubt begins to surface. You may replay a morning, a raised voice, a concession, and wonder whether steadiness really changes anything. You may also feel a small, internal ache that firmness will push your child away, or that your best efforts are invisible.

"No" is more than a word. It represents frustration, disappointment, blocked desires, delayed gratification, and unmet expectations. A child who can tolerate *"no"* is learning to handle limits, authority, peer conflict, academic challenge, rejection, and disappointment. That capacity reaches far beyond early childhood behavior and becomes a foundation for resilience across a lifetime.

Longitudinal Outcomes and Why This Matters

Decades of research point to a consistent pattern: children raised with warmth plus clear structure tend to have stronger outcomes across adolescence and adulthood. These children show lower rates of anxiety and depression, better emotional regulation, healthier peer relationships, and stronger academic performance. The combination of predictable expectations, consistent follow-through, and emotional responsiveness is what helps to produce emotionally stable and independent adults.

When boundaries are inconsistent, children often learn that escalation can change outcomes. When control is harsh and warmth is low, children may comply outwardly while carrying higher levels of anxiety or resentment. The most adaptive long-term development comes from integrating warmth and structure (Sroufe et al., 2005).

Parent exercise

- Boundary inventory: List five boundaries you enforce regularly. Next to each, mark whether you follow through *always*, *sometimes*, or *rarely*. Choose one *sometimes* boundary to make consistent this week.

Anxiety Trajectories and Avoidance

Anxiety rarely appears out of nowhere. It often grows from repeated patterns of avoidance. When a child learns that big emotions reliably makes a demand disappear, the nervous system links avoidance with relief. That relief reinforces avoidance, and anxiety can strengthen.

When big emotions are met with calm containment and the child moves through it, the nervous system encodes competence. Over time, that competence lowers vulnerability to anxiety. A calm, steady "no" does not create anxiety, it interrupts the cycle that keeps it growing.

Small exposure to try now

- Choose a low-risk stressor (waiting 30 seconds for a toy, one extra minute before a preferred activity). Use a short script, stay present, and time how long the protest lasts each day. Expect an initial spike in protest, then gradual decline.

Parent exercise

- Avoidance log: For one week, note moments when you remove a stressor to stop distress (for example, skipping a dentist visit or giving in to avoid crying). Identify one small change you can make to allow a brief, supported exposure instead.

Internal Working Models: The Blueprint of Expectation

Attachment theory describes an internal working model, a child's developing blueprint for how relationships and safety work (Bowlby, 1988). It answers questions such as: Am I safe? Are others reliable? Can I handle distress? Does connection remain during conflict?

Each calm, consistent limit paired with emotional availability updates that blueprint. The child learns that authority does not mean abandonment, conflict does not equal rejection, and strong emotions do not break the relationship. If boundaries disappear when a child escalates, the child may learn that intensity controls outcomes. If authority feels harsh or unpredictable, the child may internalize that connection is conditional.

Parent exercise

- Repair practice: After any moment you lose your temper or give in, offer a short repair: a one-line apology, one sentence about the rule, and one small reconnection (a hug, a shared joke, or a calm activity). Aim for three repairs this week and note how your child responds.

Contingency Learning: How the Brain Maps Cause and Effect

Children are constantly mapping cause and effect. They notice patterns: If I do X, then Y happens. This is how the brain learns. When escalation sometimes works, escalation becomes persistent. When calm cooperation is reliably rewarded with connection and attention, cooperation strengthens.

The important question is not whether your child is learning these patterns, but which patterns they are learning. Inconsistent boundaries teach children to push harder. Consistent and calm boundaries teach them to adapt. Over time, children begin to regulate themselves because it leads to better outcomes in their relationships.

Parent exercise

- Pattern check: For one common conflict (bedtime, leaving the park, candy requests), write the current sequence of events and the outcome. Then write the new sequence you want to create and practice it twice with a partner or in front of a mirror.

Mechanism Mapping: How Resilience Is Built

Make the pathway clear and practical:

1. Parent regulates: you slow your breath, lower your voice, and become steady.
2. Parent delivers a clear boundary: one sentence, predictable phrasing.
3. Child experiences distress: this is expected and normal.
4. Parent remains calm and connected: presence matters more than persuasion.
5. Child's nervous system recovers: distress rises and falls without catastrophe.
6. Brain encodes toleration: the child learns distress is survivable.
7. Executive function strengthens: over time, self-control improves.
8. Internal model updates: the child believes they can handle disappointment.

This is the mechanism. Resilience is not a fixed personality trait. It is built through repeated experiences in which a child feels distress, stays supported, and recovers. It begins with your ability to stay regulated.

Parent exercise

- Mechanism rehearsal: Pick one daily routine (for example, leaving for preschool). Write a three-line script for each step above and practice it aloud three times this week.

A Real Example: The Park Departure

You say *"it's time to leave."* Your child screams. You stay calm. You repeat, *"It's time to go."* They cry in the car. You remain steady. Ten minutes later, they are quiet. The next week the protest lasts eight minutes, then five, then one. Eventually they say, *"Okay."*

What changed is not magic. The child's nervous system learned the pattern: distress rises, peaks, and falls without collapse, catastrophe, or relational rupture (Shonkoff et al., 2009). That is resilience in motion.

Practical tweak to try next time

- Before leaving, offer a short regulation activity such as a two-minute heavy-work task (carrying a small bag, pushing a stroller) and a one-sentence countdown. This primes regulation and often shortens protest.

Parent exercise

- Departure drill: Role-play leaving the park with a partner. Practice the one-sentence boundary and a 60-second regulation activity. Repeat twice.

Parental Fear Revisited

Many parents worry that saying no will harm closeness. The evidence and experience say otherwise: children feel most secure when caregivers are both warm and reliably firm. Removing boundaries creates unpredictability.

Holding limits does not weaken attachment. It strengthens it. Over time, children move from *"my parent won't let me"* to *"I can handle this."* Identity begins to form around capability rather than indulgence. Children who grow up with consistent structure start to see themselves as able to manage challenges, and that sense of competence carries forward into later development.

Parent exercise

- Future self question: Write one sentence describing what you want your child to believe about themselves at age 15 when they face disappointment. Keep that sentence on your phone and read it once a day this week.

The Final Integration of HOLD

H — Hold Yourself: your regulation is the foundation.

O — Offer Accountability: model repair quickly and briefly.

L — Lead with Clarity: short, predictable phrasing reduces cognitive load.

D — Develop Resilience: contain distress long enough for learning to occur.

These are not tricks. They are developmental mechanisms. When integrated consistently, they change trajectories.

Before we close, take a breath and notice how small this work can feel in the moment and how enormous its effects are over time. The daily grind of limits and repair is quiet work. Years from now, the payoff will be a child who can sit with disappointment, who can try again after failure, who can hold a relationship steady through conflict.

Parent exercise

- HOLD script bank: Create three one-line scripts (one for each common conflict) that follow HOLD. Practice them until they feel automatic.

Two-Week Tolerance Challenge for Anxiety

Goal: reduce avoidance and increase distress tolerance through small, supported exposures.

Overview: pick one low-risk stressor (waiting for a toy, tolerating a small sensory input, leaving a preferred activity). Over 14 days, use brief, consistent exposures paired with calm containment and a simple tracking method.

Step-by-step

1. Choose the target (Day 0). Example: waiting 30 seconds for a toy.
2. Baseline (Days 1-2). Do the usual routine and time how long the protest lasts. Record it.
3. Introduce the exposure (Days 3-14). Each day, add 10–20% more tolerance time or keep the time the same and reduce parental accommodation. Use the same short script and the same calm presence each time.
4. Track: note protest length and intensity (1-5 scale) each day. Expect an initial spike in days 3-5, then gradual decline.
5. Celebrate small wins: when protest shortens or intensity drops, acknowledge it briefly: "You did that hard thing." Avoid rewards that remove the learning.
6. Adjust: if the child escalates to unsafe behavior, pause and consult a professional. This challenge is for low-risk, everyday stressors.

Daily script to use (micro-script)

- *"We'll wait here together. The plan stays the same."*

Parent exercise

- Two-week log: Create a simple table with Date | Target | Protest length | Intensity (1-5) | Parent response. Fill it out daily and review on Day 15.

Micro-Scripts Box

Use these short, fresh lines when you need a different phrasing than earlier chapters:

- *"We keep the plan. I'm here with you."* — for transitions.
- *"This is hard. We'll stay until it eases."* — for prolonged upset.
- *"Hands gentle. We pause until they are."* — for physical escalation.
- *"I'm coming back in two minutes to try again."* — when you need a brief regulated break.
- *"You did something brave. We'll try again later."* — for small wins after a failed attempt.

Tip: Say the script once, then do the steady action. The line becomes a cue, the action is the teaching.

Final Note

Keep the routines, keep the boundaries, and keep showing up. The steady acts you repeat now are the scaffolding of your child's future. In the quiet years ahead, those scaffolds become a bridge. Over time, meltdowns shorten, recovery happens faster, and your child learns *"I can handle this."*

Chapter 11

Calm and Clear Leadership in Real Life

Resilience is not built in theory. It is built in everyday routines, in the kitchen, in the car line, in the hallway at bedtime, and in the backseat after school. These ordinary moments are where calm, clear leadership is practiced and strengthened over time. You do this work in small, imperfect increments; sometimes you will feel proud, sometimes quietly exhausted, and both of those feelings are part of the story.

This chapter translates HOLD into the messy reality of family life. You will find short scripts, tiny exposures, and realistic expectations so you can lead steadily even when you are running late, undercaffeinated, or wearing yesterday's shirt.

Morning Routines: The Pressure Cooker

Mornings expose everything: limited time, competing demands, sleep deprivation, and multiple transitions. They are rarely discipline problems. They are executive function challenges under time pressure. Your child must wake from sleep, shift tasks, follow multi-step instructions, tolerate urgency, and manage sensory input. That is a lot for a developing prefrontal cortex.

What helps

- Use single-word prompts: *"Shoes," "Bathroom," "Backpack."*
- Increase visual predictability: checklist on the wall, clothes laid out, backpack packed.
- Focus on one boundary at a time. If socks are the issue, solve socks. Avoid stacking frustrations or long explanations.

When refusal happens

1. Pause and breathe.
2. Hold yourself: lower your tone and slow your body.
3. Lead with clarity: one sentence *"It's time for shoes."*
4. Offer a limited choice if needed: *"Blue shoes or black shoes?"*
5. If refusal continues, apply an immediate, logical consequence: *"We leave when shoes are on."*

Micro-practice

- Tonight: pick one morning boundary, write the one sentence you will use, and practice it aloud once.

Bedtime, Sibling Conflict, Screens, and School Resistance

Bedtime is rarely about sleep alone. It is about separation and reassurance. Wanting one more story is often a request for connection. Normalize that, then hold the structure.

- Decide the routine in advance (two books, one drink, lights out).
- State it once, neutrally: *"We read two books. It's bedtime."*
- If stalling continues, return them calmly to bed with minimal interaction and repeat the boundary.
- If you cave, repair quickly: *"I said yes when I meant no. That wasn't right. Tomorrow we'll stick to two books."*

Micro-practice

- Role-play tonight: say your bedtime script once, then act. Repeat twice.

Sibling Conflict

Sibling fights are practice for negotiation and impulse control. Your role is structure and safety, not moralizing.

- Hold yourself first. If aggression occurs, block calmly and say, *"I won't let you hit."*
- State the problem neutrally: *"You both want the same toy."*

- Use a logical containment consequence if needed: *"The toy is put away for now."*
- Coach solutions when calm and avoid shaming language.

Micro-practice

- Pick one sibling script and practice it aloud: *"Pause. What happened?"*

Screens

Screens are biologically sticky. Plan for the protest.

- Set the limit before screen time and use a timer.
- When time's up, state the transition calmly: *"It's time to turn it off."* Expect protest.
- If refusal continues, apply an immediate, related consequence: *"Screen time is done for today."* Keep consequences same day and directly tied to the behavior.

Micro-practice

- This week: use a timer for one screen session and enforce the immediate consequence if needed.

School Resistance

Ask what is driving the resistance. Is it occasional reluctance or persistent anxiety?

- For reluctance: calm, predictable boundary *"School is not optional."* Walk them in if needed.
- For persistent anxiety: collaborate with professionals and pair calm containment with gradual exposure. Avoidance reduces distress short term but strengthens anxiety long term.

Micro-practice

- Try a short exposure: one small, supported step toward the feared situation and note the child's response.

Co-Parent Alignment and Adapting These Principles to Your Family and Culture

When adults respond differently to the same behavior, children notice quickly. Alignment does not require identical personalities; it requires predictable responses. Agree on core expectations such as bedtime routines, screen limits, and how hitting is handled. Handle disagreements privately. Give other caregivers a few simple phrases they can use.

If another caregiver is inconsistent, start smaller. Aim for shared nonnegotiables rather than total philosophical agreement. Avoid criticizing other caregivers in front of the child. Outside the moment, pick one recurring issue, describe the pattern without blame, and agree on one simple response everyone can follow.

Adapting these principles to your family and culture These ideas are not one-size-fits-all. How warmth and structure look will vary across families and cultures. Having predictable limits with emotional availability can be applied universally, but the form should fit your values and context. Translate the HOLD steps into language, rituals, and routines that feel authentic in your household. If extended family or community caregivers are involved, give them a short script and a clear expectation rather than the whole framework.

Practice

- Share one script with your co-parent or caregiver this week and ask them to use it twice.

Protecting Capacity and Preventing Burnout

Your nervous system is a resource. When it is depleted, patience shortens and boundaries wobble. Capacity is a resource that needs refilling. Calm parenting depends on protecting that capacity (Maslach & Leiter, 2016).

Signs of burnout

- Dreading routine moments, increased irritability, emotional numbness, fantasizing about escape.

Protecting capacity

- Prioritize sleep if possible.
- Build support systems: friends, family, childcare exchanges.
- Define responsibilities clearly.
- Schedule regular, short periods of adult time.
- Simplify on hard days: fewer errands, simpler meals, fewer optional activities.

Tiny, realistic self-care

- One long exhale before responding.
- Drink water, sit down, or step into the bathroom for thirty seconds.
- Use brief regulation practices: a slow breath, a grounding hand on the counter, a short phrase to buy time: *"I'm going to answer you in a calm voice."*

Micro-practice

- This week: schedule one 20-minute block of adult time and treat it as nonnegotiable.

Low-Capacity HOLD

On low-capacity days, use the pared-down version:

- Hold yourself: one slow breath, lower your voice.
- Offer accountability: one sentence repair if needed, for example, *"I shouldn't have snapped."*
- Lead with clarity: one short line, for example, *"It's bedtime."*
- Develop resilience: one brief acknowledgment, for example, *"I know you're upset. It's still time."*

Steady enough is enough.

60-Second Reset

1. Pause. Stop talking.
2. Breathe: inhale 4, exhale 6, twice.
3. Lower your voice and slow your movements.
4. State one sentence boundary.
5. Hold the line for a short, decided window.

Parent Practice Plan

1. Pick one boundary to practice this week.
2. Write one micro-script and practice it aloud three times.
3. Decide your extinction-burst window (3-5 minutes).
4. Use the 60-Second Reset when you feel triggered.
5. Schedule one 20-minute recovery block for yourself.

Closing Reflection

Pause now and notice one small thing you did recently that steadied your child. Hold that memory. Over time, those small acts become scaffolding for a child who can tolerate disappointment, try again after failure, and hold relationships steady through conflict. Small meaningful moves build a lifetime of capacity.

Epilogue

The Morning with the Shoes

It's 6:03 a.m.

Snow on the ground again, the kind that makes everything feel colder than it should. I'm standing in the kitchen, lunches packed, coffee in hand. For a second I let myself remember a morning that felt like a small war with shouting, bargaining, and the slow impossible negotiations over socks.

Carter walks in. He's taller now. Still sleepy. Still slow in the mornings. But something is different.

"Time for shoes," I say.

He sighs, a small one, not a storm. He walks to the door, sits down, and pulls them on. No tears. No stomping. No kicking. Not because frustration disappeared, but because he learned how to handle it.

There were years in between: years of holding the line, years of extinction bursts, years of *"I hate you,"* years of repair, years of calm repetition when I wanted relief, years of staying steady when I wanted to collapse. The change did not happen overnight. It happened in inches: a shorter protest here, a faster recovery there, a boundary that didn't need repeating.

One morning I noticed the meltdowns were shorter. Later I realized they were less frequent. Eventually something deeper became clear: he trusted the structure, he trusted me, and then slowly he began trusting himself. That is the shift—not obedience, but capacity. Not fear, but regulation. Not silence, but strength.

Now when he grabs his backpack and says, *"Okay, I'm ready,"* I see more than cooperation. I see a nervous system that learned how to recover. I see a brain that practiced tolerating disappointment. I see a child who can hear *"no"* and remain intact. That is resilience, and it was built in ordinary moments.

Resilience rarely announces itself while it is being built. It shows up quietly later, in the child who can tolerate frustration, recover from disappointment, and keep moving forward. That quiet arrival asks a question of our culture.

We live in an era that sometimes confuses comfort with care. Modern parenting has rightly shifted toward emotional attunement; children need connection, validation, and presence. But along the way many parents began to fear something essential: being the steady authority in the room. We worried that saying *"no"* might damage attachment, that firmness might feel like rejection, that discomfort must be removed as quickly as possible. The evidence does not support that fear.

Children do not thrive when boundaries fade. They thrive when warmth and structure work together. They do not feel safest when adults negotiate under pressure. They feel safest when adults lead with clarity and steadiness. Resilience is not built by removing every obstacle. It is built by guiding children through difficulty while remaining calm and present beside them.

If we want children who can handle disappointment, constructive criticism, uncertainty, and complexity, we begin by helping them tolerate something smaller but just as important: hearing no. This is not rigidity; it is preparation.

Every sigh, every small step, every repeated boundary adds up. In those ordinary moments, resilience is being built for your child and within you as well. Pause for a moment and know that the scaffolding you place today becomes the bridge they walk on tomorrow.

Framework	Core Emphasis	Strengths	Limitations / Gaps	How HOLD Compares
Authoritative Parenting (Baumrind)	High warmth + high structure	Strong longitudinal evidence; predicts emotional regulation, academic success, lower anxiety	Broad style classification; not operationalized for daily micro-moments	HOLD operationalizes authoritative parenting into moment-by-moment leadership (regulate → clarify → contain → repair)
Triple P (Positive Parenting Program)	Behavior management, skill-building, structured intervention levels	Strong evidence base; scalable; effective for reducing behavior problems	Often program-based; may feel clinical; less focus on parent internal regulation	HOLD integrates behavioral consistency but centers parent nervous system regulation as the first step
Parent Management Training (PMT)	Reinforcement principles; contingency management	Strong outcomes for oppositional behavior; clear structure	Can feel compliance-focused; less explicit attention to emotional attunement	HOLD integrates reinforcement science but pairs it with attachment and co-regulation
The Whole-Brain Child (Siegel & Bryson)	Neuroscience-informed parenting; integration of brain systems	Accessible brain science; promotes connection and emotional literacy	Less emphasis on boundary consistency and reinforcement contingencies	HOLD integrates neuroscience but emphasizes structural clarity as regulation scaffold

Emotion Coaching (Gottman)	Validation + coaching emotional literacy	Strong support for emotional intelligence development	Risk of over-explaining; may unintentionally dilute limits if misapplied	HOLD validates emotion but limits behavior; brevity and clarity are prioritized
Gentle / Respectful Parenting (Contemporary movement)	Child-centered; relational safety; reducing shame	Strong focus on connection; counters harsh discipline culture	Often lacks clarity on consequences; may blur boundary consistency	HOLD preserves warmth but explicitly defines logical consequences and discourages next-day punishment
Attachment Parenting	Responsiveness; closeness; sensitivity	Strong early bonding focus	Less structured guidance for preschool boundary-setting	HOLD maintains attachment security while emphasizing developmental containment
HOLD Model (The Resilience Shift)	Parent regulation + clear boundaries + resilience-building	Integrates authoritative parenting, reinforcement science, attachment repair, anxiety prevention, and neurodevelopment	Not a clinical intervention model; not a substitute for individualized therapy	Focused specifically on ages 3-7; emphasizes distress tolerance, consistency under pressure, and no delayed punitive consequences

Comparison of Parenting Approaches and How HOLD Integrates and Differs

Appendix A: The HOLD Quick Reference Guide

Purpose: This guide is designed for real-life use. Not theory, not explanation, but execution. When emotions are high and your thinking brain is tired, return here.

The HOLD Model Summary

H — Hold Yourself: Your nervous system sets the tone. Before correcting behavior, regulate your body.

Do this by:

- Lowering your voice
- Slowing your movements
- Lengthening your exhale
- Pausing before speaking
- Reducing word count

Remember:

- You cannot regulate a dysregulated child from a dysregulated state.
- Your calm is the intervention.

Example: Your child refuses to put on shoes. Pause, breathe, and speak neutrally: *"It's time for shoes."*

O — Offer Accountability: Model what growth looks like. Show your child that mistakes do not undo authority or safety.

When you lose steadiness:

- Name it
- Own it
- Repair it

- Maintain the boundary

Script example: *"I raised my voice. That wasn't okay. I'm working on staying calm. The rule is still the same."*

Remember:

- Repair strengthens authority; it does not weaken it.
- Children learn that adults can handle mistakes calmly.

L — Lead with Clarity: Short. Predictable. Neutral. One sentence. No lectures, debates, or long explanations during meltdowns.

Do this by:

- Using clear, simple statements:
    - *"It's bedtime."*
    - *"The answer is no."*
    - *"I won't let you hit."*
    - *"We are leaving."*
- Pairing persistent behavior with **immediate, logical consequences**
- Keeping verbal load minimal under stress

Remember:

- Clarity reduces anxiety.
- Inconsistency increases it.
- Logical consequences are not threats—they are structure.

Example: Child refuses to turn off a screen: *"Timer's done. Screen is off."* If protest continues, enforce the consequence immediately and neutrally: *"Screen is done for today."*

D — Develop Resilience: Allow emotion, contain behavior, and stay steady.

Do this by:

- Acknowledging emotion:
    - *"I see you're upset."*
    - *"It's okay to be mad."*
- Maintaining the boundary:
    - *"The answer is still no."*
- Avoiding overcorrection:
    - Do not rescue too quickly
    - Do not add new explanations
    - Do not threaten tomorrow

Remember:

- Distress tolerated safely becomes resilience.
- Recovery is practice. Repetition builds the nervous system.

Example:

Child melts down at bedtime:

- Contain intensity neutrally
- Offer acknowledgment without negotiation
- Let distress rise and fall safely

Quick Reference at a Glance:

Step	Key Action	Parent Reminder	Example
H — Hold Yourself	Regulate first	Calm is the intervention	Pause, breathe, neutral tone
O — Offer Accountability	Repair mistakes, maintain boundaries	Repair strengthens authority	"I raised my voice. Rule is still the same."
L — Lead with Clarity	Short, neutral, consistent	Clarity reduces anxiety	"It's bedtime." Immediate consequence if needed
D — Develop Resilience	Contain emotion safely	Distress tolerated = resilience	"I see you're upset. The answer is still no."

This format is **ready to print or keep on the fridge,** to quickly scan and apply HOLD during high-stress moments without thinking through theory.

The 60-Second Reset Checklist

Use this when escalation rises — yours or your child's.

Step 1: Pause (5 sec)

- Stop talking.

Step 2: Breathe (10 sec)

- Inhale 4, exhale 6. Repeat twice.

Step 3: Lower (10 sec)

- Lower voice, slow movements, relax shoulders.

Step 4: Clarify (15 sec)

- State **one sentence boundary**. Not five.
- Example: "It's time for shoes."

Step 5: Hold (20 sec)

- Allow protest.
- Do **not** negotiate or threaten tomorrow.
- Maintain the boundary calmly.

Total: 60 seconds — You've just shifted the nervous system dynamic.

Crisis Script Template (High-Intensity Moments)

Use during public meltdowns, aggression, explosive refusal, "I hate you" moments.

Step 1: Contain Behavior

- *"I won't let you hit."*
- *"It's not safe."*
- Calm, firm, minimal words.
- "You're safe to tell me the truth. I saw what happened. Let's try again honestly."

Step 2: Name Emotion

- *"You're really mad."*
- *"You're disappointed."*
- Avoid: *"Calm down"* or *"Stop crying."*

Step 3: Restate Boundary

- *"The answer is still no."*
- Repeat if needed.

Step 4: Enforce Logical Consequence (If Required)

- Immediate, connected: *"The toy is done for today."*
- Avoid delayed punishments.

Step 5: Reconnect After Regulation

- *"I'm here."*
- *"I love you."*
- Repair, but **do not remove the boundary**.

Quick Reminders for Hard Days

- Escalation ≠ failure.
- Extinction bursts are temporary.
- Logical consequences build internal control.
- Repair builds trust.
- You are shaping **circuitry**, not just behavior.

Print Version Summary

- Calm first.
- Clear next.
- Hold steady.
- Allow feelings.
- Repair when needed.
- Resilience is built in repetition and repetition happens in ordinary moments.

Appendix B: Scripts by Age (3, 4-5, 6-7)

Calm and Clear Language for Real-Life Moments

Use this as a quick reference when emotions are high. Short. Neutral. Repeatable.

AGE 3 (Concrete thinker, high emotional intensity, short working memory)

General Guidance

- Short sentences.
- Physical proximity matters.
- Repeat instructions as needed.
- Consequences **must be immediate**.

Boundaries

- *"It's not safe."*
- *"I won't let you hit."*
- *"The toy is all done."*
- *"It's bedtime."*
- *"The answer is no."*
- **If behavior continues:**
  - *"The toy is put away."* / *"We're leaving now."*
  - **Tip:** One sentence. No lectures or explanations.

Transitions

- *"It's almost time to go."*
- *"Two more minutes."*
- *"Time to go."*
- **If refusal:** *"I'll help you."* (Pick up gently if needed.)

Public Meltdowns

- *"I see you're upset."*
- *"The answer is still no."*
- *"I'm here."*
- **If escalation continues:** *"We're going to the car."* Remove from stimulation. Minimal words.

Sibling Fights

- *"I won't let you hit."* / *"Hands down."*
- *"The toy is done."*
- Separate briefly if needed.
- **Do not force apologies.**
- Model instead: *"Try again with gentle hands."*

After You Yell

- *"I yelled. That wasn't okay."*
- *"I'm working on staying calm."*
- *"It's still bedtime."*
- Tone matters more than explanation. Keep brief.

"I Hate You" Moments

- "You're mad."
- "I love you."
- "It's still no."
- **Do not debate emotion; contain and move on.**

AGES 4-5 (Growing language, beginning perspective-taking, still impulsive under stress)

General Guidance

- Offer **limited choices**.
- Keep boundaries **predictable**.
- Begin light **coaching** after regulation.

Boundaries

- *"It's time to clean up."*
- *"You can choose blocks or books first."*
- *"I won't let you hit me."*
- *"The answer is no."*
- **If behavior continues:** *"The blocks are put away for today."* / *"Screen time is done."*
- Consequences **must be immediate and logical.**

Transitions

- *"In five minutes, we're leaving."*
- *"When the timer rings, it's time to go."*
- *"It's time now."*
- **If protest:** *"I know you want more time. It's time to go."*
- **Do not renegotiate after the timer ends.**

Public Meltdowns

- *"I see you're disappointed."*
- *"We're not buying that."*
- *"You can be mad."*
- **If escalation continues:** *"We're stepping outside."*
- **After regulation:** *"You were upset. You handled that."* Reinforce recovery, not meltdown.

Sibling Fights

- *"Pause." / "What's the problem?" / "You both want it."*
- **If aggression occurred:** *"The toy is done for now."*
- Later coaching: *"What could you say instead of pushing?"* Keep coaching short.

After You Yell

- *"I raised my voice. That wasn't okay."*
- *"The rule is still the same."*
- *"I love you."*
- Allow **brief questions**, but don't overexplain.

"I Hate You" Moments

- *"You're really mad."*
- *"I'm not going anywhere."*
- *"The answer is still no."*
- **If a child withdraws:** *"I'm here when you're ready."*

AGES 6-7 (Improved reasoning, emerging self-reflection, limited regulation under stress)

General Guidance

- Expect **more verbal pushback**.
- Stay calm through negotiation attempts.
- Invite problem-solving **after emotional intensity lowers**.

Boundaries

- *"It's time to start homework."*
- *"The answer is no."*
- *"We're leaving in five minutes."*
- **If defiance continues:** *"If homework isn't started now,*

playtime will be shorter."

- Avoid next-day punishments; link consequence to immediate behavior.

Transitions

- *"You have five minutes left."*
- *"What's your plan to finish?"*
- *"It's time now."*
- **If arguing:** *"We're not debating this. It's time."* Repeat calmly.

Public Meltdowns

- *"I can see you're upset."*
- *"We'll talk in the car."*
- *"We're leaving."*
- If your stress rises: **lower voice, shorten words**.
- Later reflection: *"That was hard. What could you try next time?"*

Sibling Fights

- *"Pause. Everyone separate."*
- *"What happened?"* / *"What's a fair solution?"*
- **If aggression occurred:** *"You chose to hit. Play is paused."*
- Encourage repair: *"What do you want to say?"* Invited, not forced.

After You Yell

- *"I lost my temper. That wasn't okay."*
- *"I'm working on staying calm."*
- *"The expectation hasn't changed."*
- Invite reflection: *"What happened to you?"* Model accountability without surrendering leadership.

"I Hate You" Moments

- *"That tells me you're really upset."*
- *"I still love you."*

- *"We can talk when you're calm."*
- Later: *"Big words come out when feelings are big."* Normalize emotion, maintain boundaries.

Quick Developmental Comparison

Age	Focus	Your Role
3	Containment	External regulator
4-5	Coaching + containment	Calm boundary + light problem-solving
6-7	Growing responsibility	Clear structure + reflection

Below is a single, consolidated **Script Bank** with unique, non-repeating lines organized by common moments. Each script is short, usable under stress, and written in your steady, warm voice.

Transitions & Leaving

- *"Shoes on now, we go in one minute."*
- *"When the timer rings, we walk out together."*
- *"Two steps to the door, then we're done."*

Morning Routines

- *"One task at a time. Socks first, then shoes."*
- *"Pick one shirt now, we'll wear it."*
- *"We leave at 7:30. That's the plan."*

Bedtime & Separation

- *"Two books, then lights out—let's pick them now."*
- *"I'll sit with you for five minutes, then lights out."*
- *"You can tell me one thing, then it's bedtime."*

Meltdowns & Big Feelings

- *"I can see this is huge for you. I'm staying."*
- *"Your feelings are loud, the rule stays the same."*
- *"Breathe with me for three counts, then we'll try again."*

Physical Escalation & Safety

- *"Hands stay gentle, we step away until they are."*
- *"I will keep you safe. We will stop this behavior now."*
- *"We take space until everyone is calm."*

Refusal & Noncompliance

- *"No is the answer today. We'll try again later."*
- *"I hear you don't want to. The plan stays the same."*
- *"You can choose how you do it, not whether."*

Sibling Conflict & Sharing

- *"Both of you get a turn; let's set a timer."*
- *"Pause. Each of you say one calm idea for solving this."*
- *"We put the toy away for a break, then try again."*

Lying (Avoidance / Honesty Support)

- "Take a breath. You're safe to tell me the truth."
- "I'm not here to get you in trouble. I want to understand what happened."
- "I saw what happened. Let's try that again honestly."
- "Thank you for telling me the truth. We'll fix it together."

Screens & Transitions from Preferred Activities

- *"Five more minutes, then we switch to something else."*
- *"When the show ends, we do a different fun thing."*
- *"Screen time is over, let's pick a new activity together."*

Repair & Accountability

- *"I lost my cool earlier. I'm sorry. Let's try again."*
- *"That didn't go well. Can we fix it together?"*
- *"I made a mistake. I'll do better next time."*

Encouragement & Small Wins

- *"You stuck with that, well done."*
- *"That was hard and you tried. I noticed."*
- *"You practiced being brave today."*

Low-Capacity / Quick Holds

- *"I need a moment, I'll be right back."*
- *"One breath, then we talk."*
- *"Short pause. We'll come back to this."*

Tip: Use each line once, then follow with a steady action (a timer, a walk, a calm touch, or a neutral consequence). The script is the cue; the action is the teaching.

Final Script Reminder

If overwhelmed, reduce to:

- *"I see you're upset."*
- *"The answer is still no."*
- *"I'm here."*

That is HOLD in language form.

Appendix C: Emotional Regulation Tools

Appendix C includes emotional regulation tools you can use both proactively and during difficult moments. These pages are designed to be simple, visual, and easy to reference when your own capacity is low. Choose one tool, practice it during calm moments, and return to it when emotions rise. Practicing one or two strategies makes the biggest difference.

PART I — Parent Self-Assessment: Your Distress Tolerance

Rate yourself: 0 = Rarely | 1 = Sometimes | 2 = Often

Tip: Lower scores = areas to grow. Patterns matter more than individual moments.

1. Tolerating Tears

- I can remain calm when my child cries.
- I do not rush to stop tears immediately.
- I can separate discomfort from danger.
- **Reflection:** Do I see tears as a threat or a developmental moment?

2. Holding Limits Under Pressure

- I maintain boundaries when escalation rises.
- I do not give in to louder protests.
- I expect escalation to decrease if I stay consistent.
- **Reflection:** Do I change the rule when pressure increases?

3. Keeping Language Clear

- I keep explanations short during conflict.
- I do not lecture or add new arguments mid-escalation.
- I repeat one clear sentence instead of debating.

- **Reflection:** Is my talking calming my child — or myself?

4. Tolerating Dislike

- I can tolerate my child being angry with me.
- I do not soften limits to avoid rejection.
- I separate approval from parenting.
- **Reflection:** Am I parenting for connection — or approval?

5. Staying Regulated Under Stress

- I notice when my voice rises.
- I can pause before reacting.
- I repair quickly after losing control.
- **Reflection:** Does urgency shrink my patience?

Reminder: Your tolerance builds your child's resilience. *Return to HOLD: H — Hold Yourself | O — Offer Accountability | L — Lead with Clarity | D — Develop Resilience*

PART II — Child Indicators of Growing Resilience

Look for trends over months, not days. Each is a sign that practice is "sticking."

Emotional Recovery *(D — Develop Resilience)*

- Meltdowns are shorter.
- Recovery happens faster.
- Child seeks connection after conflict.

Frustration Tolerance *(H/L/D)*

- Can wait slightly longer.
- Accepts "no" with shorter protests.
- Attempts problem-solving before collapsing.

- Fewer explosive reactions to small disappointments.

Reduced Negotiation *(L — Lead with Clarity)*

- Fewer repeated arguments on known rules.
- Less testing of boundaries.
- More automatic compliance in routines.

Flexibility & Transitions *(H/L/D)*

- Smoother transitions.
- Fewer extreme reactions to change.
- More willingness to try again after mistakes.

Emotional Language Growth *(O — Offer Accountability)*

- Names feelings without prompting.
- Says "I'm mad" instead of hitting.
- Expresses disappointment verbally.

Accountability Development *(O/D)*

- Attempts apologies.
- Acknowledges behavior.
- Seeks repair after conflict.

Quick Progress Check

- Small shifts = big impact.
- Example: 5-minute meltdown instead of 15, a sigh instead of a scream.
- Parental steadiness often increases *before* visible child change.
- Consistency compounds resilience.

Parent Takeaways

- Distress tolerance is not absence of emotion — it's moving through it.
- Tolerate tears, anger, frustration, and temporary rejection.
- Stay consistent. Repair quickly.
- Every steady response builds your child's capacity.

Remember:

- Calm first → Clear next → Hold steady → Allow feelings → Repair when needed.
- Resilience is built in repetition, in ordinary moments.

Let's Breathe Together

A Way to Help My Body Feel Calm

When my feelings feel big, I can use my breath
to help my body feel calm.

Trace and Breathe

Steps

1. Hold up your hand
2. Trace your hand with your finger
3. Breathe in as you go up
4. Breathe out as you go down

In...

Out

Smell the flower
(breathe in)

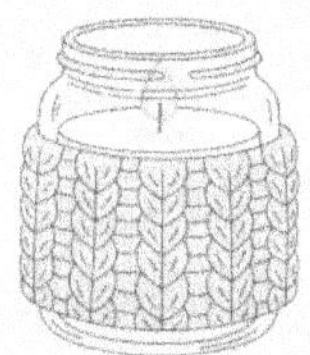

Blow out the candle
(breathe out)

When to Use This
- feelings feel big
- body feels fast or tight
- you need help calming down

Parent Tip:
Breathe with your child.
Your slow breathing helps
their body slow down too.

Move Your Body, Calm Your Mind

Simple Movement Tools for Big Emotions

Big emotions live in the body first. Before children can talk it out, they need to move it out. These movements help your child release energy, reset their body, and return to calm. Stay with your child. Model the movement. Keep your voice steady and calm.

Elephant Stomps

Stomp feet slowly and heavily on the ground.
Say: "Let's stomp it out together."
Helps with: anger, frustration, built-up energy

Snake Breathing

Take a deep breath in through your nose, slowly hiss your breath out like a snake.
Say: "Long breath in... now slow sssss out."
Helps with: calming the body, slowing breathing

Turtle Slow Walk

Walk very slowly across the room like a turtle.
Say: "Let's slow our bodies down."
Helps with: impulsivity, overstimulation

Lion Shake

Shake arms, hands, and body while making a quiet roar.
Say: "Shake it out."
Helps with: tension, frustration

Important for Parents
Your child does not need a lecture in this moment.
They need co-regulation first.
- Move with them.
- Stay calm.
- Then talk when their body is ready.

When to Use These
- Your child is overwhelmed
- Your child is yelling or hitting
- Your child is "not listening"
- Before trying to talk or problem-solve

Make It Work: Practice these when your child is calm. Use them often. Repetition builds regulation.

 # Calm-Down Corner Setup 

Create a Safe Space for Big Feelings: A calm-down corner is a quiet, safe place where children can go to slow their bodies, name their feelings, and choose a helpful strategy. This is not a punishment space—it is a support space.

What to Include in Your Calm-Down Space

Keep it simple and comforting.
Feeling Tools
☐ Feelings cards
☐ Calm-down sequence chart
☐ "How I Feel Today" page

Comfort Items

☐ Pillow or cushion
☐ Stuffed animal
☐ Soft blanket

Where to Set It Up

Choose a space that is:
quiet, low distraction,
easy for your child to access
Examples:
corner of a bedroom
small area in the living room
classroom calm space

What to Say During Big Emotions

Guide your child gently: "Your feelings are big right now." "Let's go to your calm space." "I'm here with you." Avoid forcing. The goal is to help your child learn to choose this space over time.

Regulation Supports

☐ Calm-down choice cards
☐ Breathing visual
☐ My Calm-Down Plan page

Calm-Down Tools

☐ Sensory item (fidget, stress ball)
☐ Books
☐ Headphones or quiet music
☐ Visual timer (optional)

How to Teach Your Child to Use It

Introduce the space when your child is calm, not upset.
Say: "This is your calm space. You can come here when your feelings feel big."
Practice together: sit in the space, choose a tool, take a few deep breaths

Important Reminder

The calm-down corner is **not a timeout.** It is a place to feel safe, not alone. Children learn to regulate through: connection, consistency, & practice

Parent Tip: Stay nearby when your child is learning to use this space. Over time, they will begin to use it more independently. Building this habit helps children develop lifelong emotional regulation skills.

Appendix D: Research & Citations

This book integrates research from developmental psychology, neuroscience, attachment theory, and behavioral science to support calm, clear, and consistent parenting practices. *This book is not intended to replace professional medical or psychological advice. It is designed to provide research-informed guidance to support everyday parenting decisions.*

How to Read This Appendix

This appendix includes the research, books, and professional resources referenced throughout this text. Sources are listed alphabetically by author. When available, DOIs or stable links are included to support verification and further reading.

Core Research in Development, Attachment, and Regulation

Ainsworth, M. D. S., Blehar, M. C., Waters, E., & Wall, S. (1978). *Patterns of attachment: A psychological study of the strange situation.* Erlbaum.

Belsky, J., & Pluess, M. (2009).
Beyond diathesis stress: Differential susceptibility to environmental influences. *Psychological Bulletin, 135*(6), 885–908.

Bowlby, J. (1988). *A secure base: Parent-child attachment and healthy human development.* Basic Books.

Diamond, A. (2013). Executive functions. *Annual Review of Psychology, 64,* 135–168. https://doi.org/10.1146/annurev-psych-113011-143750

Shonkoff, J. P., & Phillips, D. A. (2000). *From neurons to neighborhoods: The science of early childhood development.* National Academy Press.

Shonkoff, J. P., Boyce, W. T., & McEwen, B. S. (2009). Neuroscience, molecular biology, and the childhood roots of health disparities. *JAMA, 301*(21), 2252–2259. https://doi.org/10.1001/jama.2009.754

Sroufe, L. A., Egeland, B., Carlson, E. A., & Collins, W. A. (2005). *The development of the person: The Minnesota study of risk and adaptation.* Guilford Press.

Parenting and Developmental Frameworks

Baumrind, D. (1967). Child care practices anteceding three patterns of preschool behavior. *Genetic Psychology Monographs, 75*(1), 43–88.

Maccoby, E. E., & Martin, J. A. (1983). Socialization in the context of the family: Parent-child interaction. In E. M. Hetherington (Ed.), *Handbook of child psychology* (Vol. 4, pp. 1–101). Wiley.

Anxiety, Avoidance, and Emotional Development

Lebowitz, E. R., Omer, H., Hermes, H., & Scahill, L. (2014). Parent training for childhood anxiety disorders. *Journal of the American Academy of Child & Adolescent Psychiatry, 53*(6), 605–615. https://doi.org/10.1016/j.jaac.2014.02.015

Rubin, K. H., Coplan, R. J., & Bowker, J. C. (2009). Social withdrawal in childhood. *Annual Review of Psychology, 60*, 141–171. https://doi.org/10.1146/annurev.psych.60.110707.163642

Behavioral Science and Learning Theory

Skinner, B. F. (1953). *Science and human behavior.* Macmillan.

Kazdin, A. E. (2008). *Parent management training: Treatment for oppositional, aggressive, and antisocial behavior in children and adolescents.* Oxford University Press.

Assessment Tools

Wakschlag, L. S., Choi, S. W., Carter, A. S., Hullsiek, H., Burns, J., McCarthy, K., Leibenluft, E., & Briggs-Gowan, M. J. (2014). Defining the developmental parameters of temper loss in early childhood. *Journal of the American Academy of Child & Adolescent Psychiatry, 53*(11), 1095–1108. https://doi.org/10.1016/j.jaac.2014.07.012

Additional Information: This book translates established research into practical parenting strategies. While terminology has been simplified for accessibility, the underlying principles reflect current findings in developmental science, neuroscience, and behavioral psychology.

If you enjoyed this book, please check out my other work!

Kindergarten Readiness Workbook
Letters • Numbers • Fine Motor Skills

Big Feelings, Calm Bodies
A Guide to Help Young Children Understand and Manage Emotions

A-Z Workbook
Full alphabet tracing and phonics practice

Move Adventures Series
Interactive movement books that build listening skills, coordination, animal knowledge, and connection

Remember, leave a review online so others can find and enjoy this book too!

Macino Adventures™

Macinobookadventures.org

Scan for free exclusive bonus content

www.ingramcontent.com/pod-product-compliance
Lightning Source LLC
Chambersburg PA
CBHW050953050726
47592CB00007B/2547